AF541455

Where am I?
Who am I?

Displacement and Dislocation in *What the Body Remembers*

Axelle GIRARD

Tara Press

Where am I?
Who am I?

Axelle GIRARD

Tara Press
Flat No. 6, Khan Market, New Delhi - 110 003
Ph.: 24694610; Fax : 24618637
www.indiaresearchpress.com
contact@indiaresearchpress.com; bahrisons@vsnl.com

2007

ISBN-13 digit : 978-81-8386-019-2
ISBN-10 digit : 81-8386-019-2

Cataloguing in Publication Data
Axelle GIRARD
Where am I? Who am I?

1. Displacement 2. Diaspora 3. Punjab Culture
4. Sikhism/Sikh Culture 5. Shauna Singh Baldwin
I. Title II. Author

Printed for *India Research Press* at Focus Impressions, New Delhi.

To my parents, for their constant love and support

Acknowledgements

I am forever grateful to the people who took me to Amritsar, Bagian, Chandigarh, Jalandhar, Patiala, Sangrur and Wagah, to those who kindly welcomed me in their homes, palaces, havelis, mansions or flats in Punjab, who gave me access to their personal shrines and oratories, to their gurdwaras, showed me their holy books and their cultural relics, their traditional textiles and costumes and last but not least, who offered me a memorable taste of Punjabi cuisine.

Contents

'There will never be enough novels either by Indians or Pakistanis or by diasporic Indians and Pakistanis to tell the tales of 17 million people who became refugees as the two countries celebrated their Independence from the British.'[1]

1 Butalia, Urvashi. *The Other Side of Silence, Voices from the Partition of India*, New Delhi: Penguin Books India, 2000, p. 1.

Introduction

Following in the footsteps of Urvashi Butalia's work in *The Other Side of Silence,* Shauna Singh Baldwin's *What the Body Remembers* was greeted with no less success.

Awarded the Commonwealth Writers Prize in the Caribbean and Canada region in 2000, Baldwin's *oeuvre* was immediately considered a major contribution to contemporary Indian English fiction[2] and post-colonial literature at large. It was acknowledged as 'one of the most important and original novels about Indian history'.[3] The book was granted favourable reviews in the West, especially in England and the United States. Many critics praised it around the world. The London *Times, The New York Times Book Review* and *The Washington Post* all offered it an enthusiastic and warm welcome, as did *The Hindu.* Like novel like author, Shauna Singh Baldwin travelled the world around. Born to a Sikh family in Canada in 1962, she was brought up in India. She later studied at Marquette University to take an MBA, before marrying an Irish American. She now lives in the United States, claiming no less than three different national identities altogether.[4] Her interest in the question of language –which was highlighted in her *English Lessons and Other Stories* (1996) – stems from her own experience as a multi-cultural

2 Many novels were devoted to exploring the issues of Partition in India; most of them were published after independence, the first was Khushwant Singh's celebrated *Train to Pakistan*. But Baldwin's attempt to describe Partition from the Sikh women's point of view is a radically new idea.

3 Kevin Baldeosingh, a writer and journalist from Trinidad and Tobago, chairperson of Caribbean and Canada judging panel. Internet: www.bookfinder.com and mentioned in *What the Body Remembers*, HarperCollins Publishers India, New Delhi, 2000.

4 Internet: Soderstrom, Mary: 'From the Punjab to Montreal and Back Again': www.geocities.com/marysoderstrom/baldwin/html p. 1.

writer in the first sense. *What the Body Remembers* bears no less testimony to the author's awareness of the issues of cultural identity in the sphere of post-colonial settings at large. She is quite concerned with the influence that imperialistic forms of powers – such as colonisation, which stands as the paradigm of imperialism in *What the Body Remembers* – can have upon the ways History is told, written or made up. She is also concerned with the ways in which all forms of imperialism construct woman as gender, and the Self as a defined and immutable category within their own system.

The setting of the novel is based in Punjab, i.e. in the north-western part of British India. The story takes place during the crucial periods of pre- and post-Independence; it hinges around the event of Partition that occurred on August 14, 1947. Partition resulted in the splitting of India and the consequent creation of Pakistan, cutting through Punjab. The dividing of India is not only viewed as a historical event; it is also perceived and consequently depicted as a traumatic episode in the history of post-colonial India. It is analysed as an event that affected the country in the same way as it caused a major upheaval in the lives of millions of people. Parallels between the consequences of Partition in the microcosm or private realm and those it brought upon the public realm are numerous, stressing the impact of a geographical divide on politics and on religious communities. Partition is thus tackled as a revolution in the primary sense of the word: an event which caused a major change and led to new ways of approaching History and the location of the Self in both time and space.

It is little wonder that the story is marked by instability, and that it revolves around the issues of displacement and dislocation. Almost all the characters are depicted as ontologically divided between antagonistic entities. An upper class Oxford educated Sikh engineer and landowner, Sardarji enjoys the company of two wives, the older barren Satya and sixteen-year-old Roop. Both women provide an insight into the issue of the generation gap, which stands as one of the main themes in the novel. Satya and Roop embody two different versions of the feminine. Their struggle is symptomatic of the disorders Partition brought upon the country and people's ways of seeing (and living).

Falling into eight parts, the novel is divided into forty chapters varying in length. Starting in 1895, ending in 1965, it actually spans more than fifty crucial years as far as the reconstruction crucial to present-day India is concerned. The first part immediately follows an opening Prologue. It takes place in 1895 and consists of a brief chapter. The latter introduces the two main female characters, Satya and Roop, living in Rawalpindi. This is 1937, 10 years before Partition which is conjured up and foretold through the imagery of division. The first pages relate a silent argument between Satya and Roop. Chapter two, coming up very quickly after the beginning and opening onto the portrait of 'Vayu, bearer of perfume, god of all the Northwest of India', establishes the ongoing parallel between microcosm / macrocosm. Part two spans young Roop's life from her childhood to her marriage. Part three, counting no less than fifteen chapters covering three years (1937 to 1940) relates Roop's growing up into a woman and mother. At this stage in the novel, images of division pertaining to Partition have become clearer. Partition is made to appear as a structural matrix, governing word-play and metaphorical webs of signification, as well as characterisation. The four chapters of part four cover the beginning of World War Two, as well as Sardarji's boosted career in the Indian Civil Service. In part five, Satya leaves the stage – to come back later – and part six conjures up the difficulties of figuring out the new face of India on the eve of Partition. Part seven constitutes a transition between past/present through the exploring of Satya's reincarnation, while part eight relates the family's exodus from Punjab to Delhi in an attempt to escape from slaughter.

Beginning in Rawalpindi, within the frame of an 'Undivided India', the story of *What the Body Remembers* is to take us to independent India and to New Delhi. We, as readers, are thus made to travel in both time and space, and to approach the experience of seventeen million people whose lives were caught in a trauma. By exploring Partition through images depicting division, and by relying on themes which point to the experience of dislocation, Baldwin allows us to *sense* the protagonists' 'struggle to find a place between two cultures, one inherited and the other acquired through new education and other influences[5].' The 'struggle' Ravi mentions here is depicted in terms of a painful quest for identity, which takes on the shape of a progressive construction of the Self in *What the Body Remembers.* Readers eventually come to witness the advent of an awareness of the *I* as the *sign* of individual identity. Partition is viewed as the stage where the *I* is dis-located and displaced to the extent of having no location. The events taking place in the microcosm or private realm – namely the struggle between Satya/Roop and its symbolic implications in the diegesis – end up creating chaos within the household. Chaos later reverberates on the macrocosm as it undergoes Partition. Moreover, Roop's unorthodox attitude towards tradition reinforces the idea of a link between private/public realms, underlining the imminence of change and the growing desire for greater 'freedom' on the part of women. In fact, the main story-line, which relates the conflict between Roop/Satya, conveys the paradigmatic status of woman in the text. Females stand as the

5 Ravi, P.S. *Modern Indian Fiction, History, Politics and the Individual in the Novels of Salman Rushdie, Amitav Ghosh, Upamanyu Chatterjee*, New Delhi: Prestige Books, 2003, p. 18.

paradigm of the subject (ed.), which we shall oppose to the Self. Thus the abstract *I*, as an auto-nomous person in the etymological sense – setting its own rules for *I*tself – hides deep inside each one the female characters. The novel thus emphasises the fictional relation between character / Self. To Shauna Singh Baldwin, who has surely followed in Rushdie's footsteps, depicting history means depicting the characters *within* History and/or His-story. And she was the first author who devoted so much attention to Partition from the point of view of the Sikh community, a point of view that is often ignored or silenced. She said herself that this was the first novel which tackled the issue of Partition from the point of view of Sikh characters. Moreover, she was the first to unveil the ways in which females experienced the traumas of division. She often observed that, until *What the Body Remembers* came out, no novel had put forward the point of view of women regarding Partition:

> '...So far, we haven't read novels in English that put Sikh women front stage centre and certainly none that are about the experience of these women during Partition.'[6]

The association of women with the central idea of disorder is linked to women's perception of Partition. The fact that Baldwin should rely on particular time schemes–which do not unfold strictly linearly–shows that she establishes a connection between women / dislocation and displacement. We go from identity to dislocation, from the undivided to the divided, ending up with the picture of an obliteration and subsequent reconstruction of identity, as far as the Sikh (especially Sikh women) are concerned. The inner divisions affecting the characters become increasingly obvious as the novel

6 Shauna Singh Baldwin-Interview re What the Body Remembers: www.umiacs.umd.edu/users/sawweb/sawnet/books/SSBBordersInterviews/html p. 1

progresses, and they certainly hint at the problematic position of Sikhism in India today. It is indeed a religion that is located *in-between* Hinduism and Islamism. It is indeed a religion that comprises elements from Hinduism and Islamism, a *dislocated* religion: 'The Guru says we are neither Hindu nor Muslim' (399). The imagery of division is subsequently used as a matrix, emphasising the notion of a split identity or, rather, the notion of identity *as* division, in accordance with Weber's theory:

> 'Identity...depends upon repetition, which however, in turn, supposes something like an identity...That is to say, in order to be apprehended or identified as such–and every signifying element must be identifiable as such in order for it to signify–every signifier or 'mark' must be recognisable, repeatable. It can never present itself only once'[7].

Identity cannot be dissociated from the experience of dislocation. Geographical displacement (Partition) and the very events forecasting it are shown to be generating an identity crisis. This is why we chose to examine the signification, and implications of those two notions of dislocation and displacement.

In a figurative sense listed in *The Shorter Oxford Dictionary of English* 'dislocation' refers to a 'displacement of parts, disarrangement', and a 'disordered state', which may point here to the Self's moving towards greater individuality and subsequent 'freedom of choice'. Basically, the signification mentioned above properly applies to the idea of a disordered diegetic structure, since we saw that the novel did not follow a linear progression in time.

---

7 Weber, Samuel. *Mass Mediauras: Form Technics Media*, Stanford CA: Stanford University Press, p. 138.

Moving on to a medical sense of the word 'dislocation' that is listed in *The New Oxford Dictionary of English*, we are made to see that it may refer to an 'injury or disability caused when the normal position of a joint or other part of the body is disturbed.' Basic connotations of physical dislocation can be found within the text, where some characters' physical disabilities metaphorically point to the invalidity of imperialism as well as to its traumatic consequences upon the Self.

Turning to *The Oxford English Dictionary*, we came across the signification of the verb 'to dislocate', which is said to be the equivalent of throwing something 'into confusion or disorder, upset, disarrange, derange, disconcert'. Changes occurring within the narrative voice may indeed apply to that signification. All those definitions establish an ongoing diegetic link between physical displacement and changes occurring within the characters. The repeated illustration of dislocation in *What the Body Remembers* somehow brings to mind Jacques Derrida's idea of literary 'iterability', which he defines as repetition-with-a-difference as it 'implies both repetition and difference'[8].

To *The New Oxford Dictionary of English* now, displacement means 'the removal of someone or something by someone or something else which takes their place.' It obviously implies consecution, i.e. fact(s) followed by (a) consequence(s). The displacement, i.e. the re-placing of a given pattern at various stages in the text – provides us with the most visible symptom of displacement as it is defined here. Now, *The Webster's Revised Unabridged* (on the web) equates the meaning of 'displacement' with that of 'translation', i.e. the displacing of an element

8 Derrida, Jacques. 'Limited Inc a, b, c...', trans. Samuel Weber, *Glyph* 2, 1977, rpt. in *Limited Inc*, trans. Samuel Weber and Jeffrey Mehlman, Evanston IL: Northwestern University Press, p. 53.

pertaining to one setting into another. That one definition clearly fits with the aesthetics hybridisation Baldwin often resorts to in *What the Body Remembers*.

Dislocation and displacement are thus understood, and subsequently dealt with as physical phenomena, reverberating on the literary treatment of History. The 'body' that is highlighted from the title onwards, provides the author with the very support of change taking on the shape of dislocation and displacement. It fact, it is especially the female body which is driven to be the *locus* of a paradoxical metamorphosis, i.e. the place where repetition meets difference and where identity is finally provided with a construction. The female body is viewed as an organ commanding the transposition and transformation of the Self as that 'infinitised' *I* which 'proliferates in mimetic, fictional, connoted objects'[9] transcending the polarities of male discourse and its subsequent limitations.

Baldwin approaches the Self through its relations with History, religion, culture and politics. The Self is considered a result of a number of attempts to define it, within the frame of imperialistic thought and discourse, in the way which Edward Said defined it:

> 'The will to exercise dominant control in society and history...a way to clothe, disguise, rarefy and wrap itself systematically in the language of truth, discipline, rationality, utilitarian value, and knowledge'[10].

9 'Women and Literary Space', in Navati, U.M and C. Kar, Prafulla. *Rethinking Indian Literature in English*, Delhi: Pencraft International, 2000, p. 96.

10 Said, Edward. *The World, the Text, and the Critic*, Cambridge, M.A: Harvard University Press, p. 216.

The author's aim, we think, was to provide readers with an insight into the ways through which the post-colonial Self actually constructs *I*tself, within the frame of geographical, cultural and religious dislocation. She intended to counter the polarities regulating imperialistic systems of representation: male/woman, same/other in order to display a construction of the self on a metaphorical basis.

I – The Body Divided

Self, Function and Subjection

From the very beginning of the novel, Baldwin's characters seem to be caught in a network of possible (in) determinations in the ontological sense. The opening 'Prologue' confronts readers with a voice appearing under the shape of an indeterminate *I* whose origin we have no clue about. 'I have grey eyes in this lifetime and they are wide open as I am severed from my mother's womb.' (11) This Prologue provides the *I* with its primary essential indeterminacy: *It*, the Self is assimilated to something that appears to be unattainable as it is compared with 'the futility of tears' (11), i.e. with the idea of something fluid that is hard to get a grip on. What is more, the expression of movement is caught in a network of antitheses conveying the ideas of paralysis and circularity. The finite verb 'falls' is immediately countered by the word 'climb', while the idea of a progression that is expressed by the verb 'learn' is counterbalanced by the idea of backward movement as suggested by the verbs 'slip-slide back' and 'resume'. Though *It* is named in the very beginning, the *I* cropping up in the Prologue cannot actually be identified for it does not refer to a specific character. It reveals *It*self as absence proper: 'I <u>am not a</u> boy'. (11) The recourse to three successive dots stretching between the word 'again' and the rest of the sentence ('born a woman') emphasises the central idea of absence and allows the narrator to connect it to womanhood: being a woman is *not being* a man.

Being, or the person, is either undetermined, or associated with something it is not – within the frame of a sexualised ontology. Women are thus *originally* confined to the realm of the invisible. The image of the circle figuratively replays the idea of unidentified origin. It launches the recurring imagery of circularity pervading the novel, and introduces the symbolic value of the apricot that is to be found on page 15. The fruit is referred to by a synecdoche designating it as a 'stone' and connoting the impenetrability of origin. The idea of opacity is further highlighted through the emphasis the author lays upon images of interiority: Satya is said to have a clear vision and knowledge of 'herself' inside. She 'hears laughter answering her' (15) and eventually proves unable to deceive her own self. The verbs 'sees', 'examines' (16) and 'watch' (17) are all part of a figural illustration of the circle motif, and they allow the author to associate the ideas of absence (or woman as absence) with that of introspection.

Page 15, the sentence displaying 'Roop's features, her Pothwari skin, smooth as a new apricot, beckoning from the limb of a tall tree' (15) establishes a connection between the image of the apricot and the idea of fertility. Roop's youth is compared to the ripeness of the 'new' apricot which, as a fruit, refers to the idea of *bearing* fruits like one bears children. This is why Satya, a barren woman, fails to ingest the apricot; her body cannot receive life because it cannot give it. Satya cannot do her duty as she cannot perform the function of women, i.e. giving birth. Satya 'spat the stone out' (23). The association of the apricot with the 'womb' is underlined in an enumeration –her 'mouth', her 'womb', her 'gullet', her 'lungs' (23)–confirms the idea of an equivalence between woman/body and body/function. On page 529, the association of 'women and children', both compared to 'apricots', clearly shows that women are meant to give life. That is the only way for them to be recognised *as* women. Thus it is little wonder that Satya finally ends up being excluded from the realm of the living.

Later in the text, it appears that the narrator's focalisation on Kusum's 'womb' – which has been 'ripped out' (511) – points to the association of the ideas of woman and childbearing. It also suggests the dislocation of woman as body and her subsequent annihilation. If women decide to reject function, i.e. if they refuse or simply fail to do what they are expected to do, then they will have to pay a high price for it. We have observed already that Satya had to take her own life as a result of her serial dysfunctions. Page 117, Roop's attempt at walking back home alone with her horse Nirvair actually ends up by her own metaphorical exclusion from the realm of the living. Soon enough, all familiar landmarks in the landscape are shown to be fading away: verbs connoting vision in the passage are associated with the expression of uncertainty and indeterminacy. The adverb 'perhaps', together with the words 'anyone' (118) and 'no one' all convey the idea of a blurring of boundaries. Roop does not know where she is any more. She is being 'alone' for the first time. Having physically gone astray, she has metaphorically transgressed the limitations intrinsic to her function, i.e. she has not followed the rules she should have as little girl and future woman. The syllepsis on the word 'distance' (both physical and symbolic) suggests transgression in both proper and figurative senses.

While women are associated with the idea of impenetrability, men are often associated with that of division. Bachan Singh is a landowner striving against those who would be ready to deprive him of his possessions (namely, his Hindu half-brother Shyam Chacha), and Sardarji is a canal-engineer, symbolically digging into the earth to control its moves. Page 184, Sardarji has been promoted and 'now he goes after building a few dams, planning a few canal systems, as Executive engineer', contributing in his way to the country's Partition. Page 268, the reference to the 'canal colony house' that is divided into two parts, one inhabited by Satya and the other by Roop reinforces the idea of the male colonising the female through His own activity, reducing Her to function. Male characters are those who separate and divide: 'I have let my family walk the border between one faith and the other', Bachan Singh says, page 68. Designing 'a new plan' (100) for his daughters, their Papaji makes the decision that they will 'attend a boarding school for Sikh girls, Bhai Takht Singh's school', a distant place, 'a place with walls twelve feet high so they'll be insulated from all the anger brewing in Punjab' (100-101)[11]. A 'school with chairs for Roop and walls twelve feet high' (101) to prevent the (female) students from running away. The image of confinement also hints at the new boundaries that will be set by the future Partition of India.

The counterpart to men's domination of boundaries lies in their incapacity to see. Men's seemingly visionary gaze still lacks the capacity to see and seize the intrinsic identity of things and selves around them. Playing around with her brother Jeevan, Roop happens to stand up to him and be stronger: 'She should have

11 Note that the imagery of impenetrability will be taken up later, to describe the scenery in Jallianwala Bagh.

been less strong, that was it.' (35) Deciphering her brother's impalpable dismay as she watches and attempts to interpret his ways and reactions, Roop realises she should have pretended to be less strong. The scene is filled with words resorting to the semantic field of seeing – 'glance', 'watches'. Roop is obviously looking for 'clues' to interpret her brother's puzzling expression, her gaze seeks to grasp the meaning of another's gaze, of another's face, of the Other. What first seems to be something 'Abrupt. Disapproving', soon becomes something the girl proves able to understand. 'She gives Jeevan a smile. He smiles back. All is well again.' (35). Like Roop, Satya is endowed with the capacity to observe and see through things and men around her. On page 26, she stresses her ability to 'see' what is 'inside' her husband Sardarji. Like Roop, Satya sees and therefore she knows. 'Yes, I know you, know you better than you know yourself,' she stresses on the same page. Later on she confirms: 'I tell you what I see inside you, that's why you throw me away.' (166). '*Let's stop pretending we know one another,*' she says on page 456, claiming that Sardarji never knew her the way she did him for he has never *seen* her. Men's way of looking at women is superficial, because they content themselves with looking at them 'from the corner of their eyes. Their eyes are like horses' eyes: they do not see what lies directly before them' (64).

As they fail to see, men run the risk of becoming blind. 'I have been blind, Bachan Singh ironically suggests (60). Page 45, the allegoric partridges' contest provides us with a parodic image of men's blindness: 'eye to eye, at the centre of the circle of men' (45), the partridges probably fight because they fail to see what they should do otherwise. The partridges' fighting scene provides the narrator with the opportunity to reverse the order of sexual partition: the 'circle' designates a metaphorical gathering of women watching blind men fight. The image of the circle had been associated with women earlier. It is now being associated with men, who are being looked at by women, i.e. subjected to the women's gaze. Surprisingly enough, Pavan's 'different way of seeing' (382) is akin to the men's. The child fails to recognise her mother as such, deeming Satya to be that mother. Pavan '*seems also to see like a man*' (271). Atman Singh, on the contrary, was trained by Satya to read 'his master's 'every gesture and know his deeds' (173). To women, vision is observation, and it is linked to memory. For men, vision is caught within the immutable fixity characterising imperialistic systems of representation; and each gender has its particular ways of looking at the past.

Ethics and History

It is little wonder that the idea of memory should chiefly be associated with women. Females are indeed considered the guardians of tradition. They are meant to teach and pass on the principles and customs governing society to future generations, so as to make sure traditional values will prevail as they did in the past. Memory is endowed with a political function within the private realm, a space belonging to women since the public one is governed by men. The sexual partition of space one may decipher in *What the Body Remembers* reveals some sort of trans-cultural reality: Aristotle's *polis* – public space – was already revolving around a sexually divided space, separating men from women. Thus one may easily understand that:

> 'The freedom achieved outside the domestic enclosure was purchased at the risk of ostracism, or at best marginalisation while paradoxically a central position in society – as a wife or mother – could be granted to only those who submitted to the collective feminine code of conformity which erased the individual self'[12].

12 Mukherjee, Meenakshi. *The Perishable Empire, Essays on Indian Writing in English*, New Delhi: Oxford University Press, 2000, p. 78.

The importance of memory within the frame of political, social or religious constructions is conveyed through the numerous references of the past as a didactic element. The Prologue states: '*And if you do not learn what you were meant to learn from your past lives, you are condemned to repeat them.*' (11). Juxtaposing the expression 'past lives' and the verb 'repeat', Satya stresses the link which binds the past to the present. Time is dislocated proper, since the mind of the Self as subject is systematically encouraged to look into the past, in order to find proper responses for *now*. History itself could not be interpreted, let alone told without 'memory'. Page 61, Bachan Singh's mention of Jallianwala Bagh soon becomes a pretext for the exposition of that tragic event, covering pages 62 to 65.

In fact, 'memory' provides Baldwin with a pretext for disturbing 'regular' time schemes. Memory intervenes through 'its little props, insertions from the past, the silent evidence of other times' bringing 'old selves crowding to the fore, casting their shadow across the shadows of the waking mind' (208). Almost every event that is retraced in the novel provides the author-cum-narrator with an opportunity to *refer* to something past. When Roop's dying Mama strives 'to remember how it felt to die, in order to repeat the process', (76) Satya obviously chooses to ignore the didactic dimension of the past. She consequently fails to make improvements regarding her present life: 'Distance contracts between another time and this, memory bringing before her all the actions she repeats in this life – oh, Satya never learns, never improves her karma' (193-194).

The didactic value of time past, i.e. what one is liable to learn from past experience is suggested by the idea of connection between now/then. The link between past/present is sometimes embodied by the use of hyphens, putting two words together in order to make one out of those. For instance, the recurring expression 'what-women-are-for' suggests the eternal value of the verb 'are'. Women 'are' not: they 'are-for' something specific, i.e. they are something on the condition that they meet with males' requirements. But using a hyphen may also allow the narrator to voice the discrepancy between what is required from women/what women desire for themselves. Thus the narrator may also rely on the use of hyphens to voice a sense of ironic distance regarding *traditional* discourse, i.e. males' discourse on what woman should 'be'.

"L'ironie, qui ne craint plus les surprises, *joue* avec le danger (...) l'ironie va le voir, elle l'imite, le provoque, le tourne en ridicule, elle l'entretient pour sa récréation."[13]

Page 79, the narrator's destruction of the sacred aura surrounding the cow (in Hinduism) through the use of repetition, pointing to debunking of traditional discourse, thus proceeds from a logic of ironic subversion. The word cow is repeated no less than four times within a space of eight lines – a means of stressing its sacred significance to the extent of parody: 'Bring cow's urine', 'So sacred is the cow', "I'll make you go to the cow compound to get the cow urine!" (79). As for the Sikhs the cow is not a holy animal, the narrator's comment : 'So sacred is a cow' appears to be loaded with irony. One may observe that the subversion of traditional discourse has become a frequent feature in contemporary Indian English fiction. Subversion applies to myths, beliefs or customs

13 Jankélévitch, Vladimir. *L'Ironie*, Paris: Flammarion, 1964, p. 11. "Irony, as it no longer fears surprise, actually plays with fire (...) irony provokes danger, imitating it, arousing it, deriding it, playing with it..."

one is liable to come across when studying modern Indian fiction, and often takes on the shape of ironic distance between what is said (or written) / what is meant. We all remember Rushdie's reduction of the great *Ramayana* to Saleem's own great personal narrative in *Midnight's Children*. Is not the allusion to Indra's churning of matter given comic tones when compared with Saleem's upset stomach?

Duality and Structure

Ironic displacement works in the same ways as Memory, i.e. within the frame dislocation. Like tradition, structure appears to be disordered or essentially dismembered. Two levels of temporality are juxtaposed within the frame of a single narrative, exposing duality as a process that is akin to the very idea of reincarnation. We might go as far as to say that the disruption of time schemes – or the clash between present narrative/narratives from the past – bears testimony to the pervading idea of reincarnation. The theme of reincarnation is launched from the Prologue onward. Presenting us with a Satya speaking on her coming into the world as a woman claiming she has 'slid down the snake's tail', coming back as 'a woman' (12), the Prologue immediately makes the idea of reincarnation an important part of the setting. It also associates the image of the female womb – what Panja calls 'woman's notion of cyclical rather than linear time'[14]– with the idea of re-generation and consequent metamorphosis, an image which possibly accounts for the problematic identity of *What the Body Remembers* as far as the notion of *genre* is concerned. The text is consequently marked by a sense of mobility and openness.

---

14 Panja, Shormistha. 'Women and Literary Space', in Navati, U.M. and Prafulla, C. Kar. *Rethinking Indian English Literature*, New Delhi: Pencraft International, p. 95.

This is the story of a polygamous marriage, dominated by the rivalry of two main female characters embodying two ways of seeing on the eve of Partition. Is that a historical novel then? Not only. It also fits in the category of the *roman d'apprentissage*, if one chooses to focus on the retracing of Roop's evolution from youth to motherhood, or on Sardarji's coming to terms with his problematic identity. Short Chapter 20 (239-243) is important in this respect, as it confronts readers with the otherwise silent character's inner thoughts on the basis of zero focalisation: 'He can see he will have to put his foot down some day; overcome his natural kindness' (242) the narrator guesses, watching its[15] own character's actions. Last but not least, the novel could be labelled feminist, provided that hypothesis be based on Baldwin's own definition of feminism:

> 'If you define feminism as the radical notion that a woman is a person – it depends on how accustomed you are to women having rights as people, including the right to own their body...Nevertheless, the men in this novel are also trapped in their gender, religion, times and cultures too'[16].

The very notion of (literary) genre is challenged in *What the Body Remembers* – thanks to the generic plurality of the novel which the author bases upon a sense of modernity as she claims: 'I dislike the business of categorising writers...categories abound, and I'd like to point out how inappropriate are the old categories, before

15 The question of his / her (?) sexual identity being an open one, we chose to use the personal pronoun 'It' to refer to the narrator.

16 Bold Type: Essay by Shauna Singh Baldwin, Internet:www.randomhouse.com/boldtype/1199/baldwin/essay/html.

my novel is thrown into one'[17]. Genre is no longer approached as a monolithic space, but rather as a dual one. And what happens to genre occurs within the narrative voice as well. The narrator indeed jumps from one mode to the other as far as discourse is concerned, i.e. the act of telling something through saying or writing something – blurring the boundaries between speaker/writer. One is sometimes given a similar impression as that which Edward Said experimented with in reading *Kim*:

> 'Whether we like the fact or not, we should regard its author as writing not just from the dominating viewpoint of a white man describing a colonial possession, but also from the perspective of a massive colonial system'[18].

Splits governing the category of genre obviously play a central role in *What the Body Remembers*. Distortions affecting the narrative from the point of view of structure can also be related to the question of History. It has been suggested already that Baldwin had intended to write a new version of Partition. Like Urvashi Butalia with *The Other Side of Silence*, she sought to reveal hidden truths, silent ways and voices from Partition. She strove to reach for a 'reappropriation of history' on the grounds of fiction.[19] We shall now try to grasp the ways in which *What the Body Remembers* constituted an attempt to reformulate History on the part of the author-cum-narrator.

---

17 Shauna Singh Baldwin-Interview re What the Body Remembers, Internet: www.umiacs.umd.edu/users/sawweb/sawnet/books/SSBBordersInterview.html, p. 1.

18 Said, Edward, W. 'Preface' to *Kim* by Kipling, Rudyard. London: 1901, London: Penguin 1989, p. 9.

19 The idea of a '*reappropriation of History*' is a major and a widely explored one in the works ranging in what is now refered to as modern Indian English fiction. It therefore testifies to the traumatic effects of Partition in India, and confirms many a contemporary authors' concern with the need to rebuild history and country after Partition.

Proceeding to the revision of official History through the strategic debunking of imperialistic discourses about Partition, Baldwin has achieved a subversion (and sub-version) of official History, relying on the imagery of dislocation and displacement. Describing Kusum's horridly dismembered body towards the end of the book the narrator says it bears a 'message' (515). Obviously enough, the image of a mutilated body needs deciphering. It is therefore associated with an idea of the impenetrability of historical truth and is certainly located on the dark side of official History. It appears from this that the body remains the only source of possible memory; it is the place where to look for the past, the *locus* enclosing the unspoken realities of what *was*. Baldwin's concern with History appears quite clearly when the author-cum-narrator conjures up Bachan Singh's decision to forbid his family to go to the Hindu temple. Every member of the family seems to relate to Hindu divinities in their own way; Revati Bhua, we are told, only talks to Lakshmi. She never addresses Vaheguru, the Sikhs' holy name for God. Roop and Madani enjoy listening to Pandit Dinanath's reading of the *Ramayana* (56), while their father resents the possible influence Hindu mythology might have on his daughters. His fear reveals the link which binds story/truth, History/truth in the novel as far as the question of religious truth is concerned. When forbidding the women to attend the Hindu temple, Bachan Singh acts as a *coloniser* proper. He establishes a parallel between stories (myths)/History, and intends to choose the very contents of History himself. He ironically fails to protect the memory of his qom by wanting too much to preserve it. A few pages later, the narrator binds History to masculine hegemony, by restricting the space of story-telling to the circle of men. Page 61, Bachan Singh and Jeevan are alone when discussing the events of Jallianwala Bagh: Roop is simply struggling 'to keep her eyes open' and is only 'half listening' (62). She makes 'no answers' (63) to her father's questions, while the other female in the room (Revati Bhua) snoozes and 'sighs' (65). The female characters' way of telling History significantly takes on the shape of 'lori rhymes' (lullabies), 'janam-sakhis' (commemorative songs on Guru Nanak's life written in the second half of the 17th century). But women have their own special way of relating to the past. Moving to the contents of the conversation between father and son, one cannot help being struck by the way in which the semantic field of confinement actually pervades the text. Next to 'the back walls' (62) of 'haveli compounds' are those 'very high' 'parts of the wall'. The narrowness of the place is emphasised a little farther, suggesting the necessary, yet difficult unveiling of History. The heart-to-heart father-son conversation when Bachan Singh depicted the people at Jallianwala Bagh, 'some talking, laughing, playing cards, telling stories, some listening to speeches' (62) also suggests the possible transmission of historical truth.[20]

History is no longer approached as anecdote; it is closely linked to the story of characters and reveals the importance of Memory within the frame of the construction of the Self. The ways in which the Self deals with History is in many ways reminiscent of Nietzsche's definition of the 'super-historical' mode of historical consciousness. Having discussed three possible ways of coming to terms with the past, Nietzsche defined an 'unhistorical' mode of consciousness, within the frame of which the Self literally 'gets rid' of the past in order to live on the present. The second mode he defined was called 'historical' and meant to designate the subject's

20 On April 13, 1919, General Dyer ordered his Gurkhas to shoot at the crowd of Indian demonstrators (20 per cent Sikhs) who protested British repression of nationalist activities assimilated to 'activity by an external enemy'.

ability to accept official, conventional History, i.e. with the past re-presented as it is. Last but not least, the third mode he defined was the 'super-historical', which referred to a specific historical consciousness since it would not dissociate History from the Self within the very representation of the past (or History). Bachan Singh seems to re-think the events of Jallianwala Bagh in a way that is akin to Nietzsche's 'super-historical' mode of historical consciousness. The Self is perceived as a creator proper: accusing the 'English magistrate' on page 63, he claims that 'he lies'. According to Bachan Singh, there were no less than 'two thousand bodies' lying on the ground, not just 'four hundred' (63) as assessed by the colonisers.

II – The Body Dismembered

Divided by a Common Language

Language provides Baldwin with a field of predilection: the distortions that can be observed within speech are symptomatic of the author's will to depict the link binding division to dismemberment. Language is, so to say, a sign revealing the dislocation of the Self within the frame of a colonial (and probably post-colonial) setting.

While the main narrative is given in English, Baldwin occasionally inserts words in Punjabi, Hindi or Urdu. Those embody the presence of the Other as it is perceived in the eye of colonisers as the Indian-other as opposed to the English. The use of language variance is twofold as it does not only aim at exposing the reification of the Indian-other by the colonisers: it also provides the author-cum-narrator with the opportunity to celebrate Sikh culture. Words revealing Baldwin's belonging to the Sikh community are seldom translated. The author-cum-narrator obviously wishes to encourage her readers to be curious enough to look up unknown meanings themselves. It is little wonder though, that the absence of translation should generate a sense of disorientation among Western readers. Following in the footsteps of other Indian English writers, certainly aimed at providing her Western readers with a sense of linguistic dislocation usually experienced by the colonised. Giving vent to lengthy descriptions of Parsi religious customs, prayers, costumes and funeral rites in *Such a Long Journey* and confronting Western readers with words like: '*dugli, Behram roje, dustoor, navjote*', Rohinton Mistry no doubt created a similar sense of disorientation. Like Baldwin, he subverted the categories of centre / periphery in order to have the (former) coloniser experiencing what used to be the dislocation of the colonised. Estrangement is no longer felt by the prototype of the colonised (the Punjabi or Hindi reader) but by that of the coloniser (the Western readership). *What the Body Remembers* is replete with words pertaining to Sikh culture. It is clear enough that the author sought to provide her readers with specific information concerning her characters' (and incidentally her) own religious background. The realities of Sikhism no doubt remain a mystery to many of us in the West. Page 51, Roop's Mama cremation scene is depicted with meticulous attention. The 'Guru Granth Sahib' – the Sikhs' holy book – is mentioned on page 50: "Sing me a shabad, Roop" (50), while the dying mother is pictured as a praying and pleading woman. Surprisingly enough, the following sentence: 'Mera vaid Guru Gobinda' (50) and the following word 'vaqt' (51) are actually translated. Farther, the word 'atma' is not translated but its Greek cousin, 'atmos' may help Western readers not familiar with Hinduism to grasp the meaning of it. Later, the listing of the five pillars of Sikhism, 'the five Ks (57) introduces us into the reality of Sikhism. Let us jot down that the Five Kakkars refer to men's five duties: wearing a bracelet (*kara*), wearing a beard and not cutting their hair (*kesh*), wearing short pants (*kachcha*) and carrying a sword (*kirpan*) as well as a comb (*kanga*). By offering readers cultural information on Sikh ways and customs, Baldwin provides us with an insight into her own culture: Other becomes Author in the event of descriptive digressions, contributing to the building up of a space that is devoted to the construction of otherness, by slowing down the speed of the narrative. Reviving Sikh culture through literature, Baldwin sought to underline the persistence of it: page 148, she tells us that in the gurdwara, the Sikh temple, 'There is Sardar Kushal Singh and his brother-in-law, the 'boy' in this wedding, forty-two-year-old Sardarji' (148), using the present tense as a means of suggesting continuity. Later on page 149 comes the recitation of 'Lavaan', a word that refers to the circumambulations of the faithful around the Guru Granth Sahib as an essential part of the wedding ceremony. The narrator's mention of the daily Ardaas, which are performed in remembrance of all the Gurus and of the martyrs 'from Mughal times' (146), pointing to the history of Sikhism, namely that of the Gurus who refused to convert to Islam in spite of the rules promulgated by Mughal emperors.

Language variance also comes under the shape of mixing. Taking words from both English and Indian languages, the narrator produces fusion within syntax. The following coinage: 'what-people-will-say' offers a striking example of language variance. It juxtaposes a number of words in English, but those words are not lined up the way they should according to grammar. The 'sentence' may be understood, and what is more, it may be heard quite often. But the correct, normative structure has been inverted at the expense of *English* grammar; an inversion which results in the expression of a written-colloquial language. What is at stake here is the dismemberment of normative language within the frame of a reversal of values, displacing centre onto periphery and vice-versa. The repetition of the adjectives 'good' and 'sweet' in the following coinage: 'good-good sweet-sweet Sikh woman' (124), also points to a sense of colloquialism, and to oral speech at large. The language of the centre is handled in a way that is liable to throw Western readers into confusion, in the way that the colonised were disoriented when confronted to the coloniser's language within the frame of imperialism. Thus, the use of hyphens could embody the very sign of dismemberment, as a reaction to former imperialistic attempts at homogenising and possibly annihilating the Other as such, which Mukherjee referred to as 'a greater pull towards the homogenisation of reality' 'in the English texts of India' (12). To conclude this part of our discussion, we would like to quote Rushdie's vision of language variance:

> 'I hope all of us share the opinion that we can't simply use the language the way the British did; that it needs remaking for our own purposes. Those of us who use English do so in spite of our ambiguity towards it, or perhaps because of that, perhaps because we can find in that linguistic struggle a reflection of other struggles taking place in the real world, struggles between the cultures within ourselves and the influences at work upon our societies. To conquer English may be to complete the process of making ourselves free'.[21]

Besides the juxtaposing of different languages within the frame of linguistic dislocation, Baldwin occasionally resorts to the use of a polyphonic narrative voice, mingling various speeches and / or discourses within the same passage. Shifting from one type of narration to the other, from zero focalisation – 'If Sardarji had not expressed his will, she would not have shared her daughter

21 Rushdie, Salman. *Imaginary Homelands*, New York: Granta, 1992, p. 17.

with Satya, so selfish and ungrateful she had become' (226) – to interior monologue – '*I am not good-good enough for all he has done for me. If I am not careful, everyone will say let her be alone*' (226) – the narrator superimposes two different discourses. Moreover, the passage quoted above is all the more striking as it voices two different points of view emanating from the *same* character. In the above sentence, Roop's inner rage is clearly counterbalanced by her superego taking on the shape of traditional discourse. Page 82, Nani advises Roop: 'Listen and obey your father': voicing Roop's inner thoughts a few lines further, it unveils the girl's will to comply with set rules. '*There should be no difference between one and the other*' (82). Dialogism, i.e. the superimposition of conflicting speeches within the narrative voice also provides a field for competition between the coloniser/the colonised. Voicing each of the two female characters' speech in turn on page 430, the narrator conveys the idea of some sort of contest taking place between the coloniser/the colonised. 'If Miss Barlow has her way any longer, Roop's children will be hers', the narrator reflects, voicing Roop's inner thoughts. They are countered in turn through the expression of her adversary's inner speech: 'There are so many ways to take away children' (430). Language definitely provides the characters with a field for competition; standing for the colonisers', Miss Barlow embodies an imperialistic will to power Roop can only strive to counter. In fact, the governess's subversion of the children's names she has made English, confirms that language constitutes a ground for the exercise of colonial imperialism. The removal of Timcu's turban from his head – i.e. the sign bearing testimony to his belonging to the Sikh community – by Miss Barlow, who has got rid of it in favour of those 'placards' dangling down the children's necks and bearing two English names made up for them, is a metaphor for the colonisers' annihilation of the (colonised) Self. 'Pavan's says 'Joan'', and 'Timcu's says 'Edward'' (429).

In making plain the terms of the contest between coloniser/ colonised from a linguistic point of view, Baldwin achieved a reversal of values. Centre undergoes systematic challenge from periphery. Bachan Singh's 'limited English' is not presented as a defect for he is said to be writing 'Punjabi well' as well as 'Persian and Gurmukhi scripts' (43).

Janus-faced Characters

The disfigurement of language finds a corollary within the almost tangible dismemberment of characters in *What the Body Remembers.* Assuming that Roop and Satya are the two main women characters, standing for the re-presentation of woman proper, we shall be led to question the presence of a complementary couple of protagonists. In choosing to have two main female characters the author sought to divide, and consequently dismember woman as gender. Satya and Roop are two versions of the same woman within the frame of characterisation. This is made all the more clear as they each have different ways of reacting to what affects them in the text. It was said already that Satya rather stood for the (problematic) representation of tradition, while Roop belonged to another generation, seeking greater freedom and a revision of the sexual partition governing the roles of men and women. Although she cannot help criticising Sardarji and the men around her, Satya still stands for subjection. The elder wife makes no secret of her intention to 'show Roop an example' (193) for 'example creates fear' and 'fear keeps control' (193). She intends to raise the younger wife whose duty, she thinks, consists in 'Nothing but bear fruit' (195). Barren Satya and fertile Roop are one, for 'Satya still needs Roop for what Roop's body can do' (195). To Satya, second wives like Roop should just behave like those 'in all the Sind-Sagar doab, that land that lies between the Indus and its sister river, the Jhelum, where women are raised to bend like saplings, with every wind so long as it speaks with a voice of authority' (20). The elder wife observes that she and Roop are poles apart regarding the legacy of tradition: 'Young women these days think they are invincible, that they have only to smile and good things will happen to them' (18). Satya is often shocked by Roop's behaviour and the way she appears to take everything for granted: 'How can Roop take anything Sardarji gives, even the last pinni sweet on his plate, as evidence of his love?' (193). Though Satya keeps '*her eyes wide open*' (12) and '*will never lower them before a man*' (12), she requests the opposite from Roop. Satya and Roop resent the power of men. Roop's conspicuous femininity can thus be interpreted as a sign of resistance against men. Moving 'without haste, with a full-bottomed deliberateness', 'she is a top slowing and bobbing to rest' (192). Her moves are depicted as slow, and seem endowed with a sense of carelessness which somehow goes against the validity of the link males have been shown to establish between woman/function (childbearing). It should be observed that the girl's stomach–a synecdoche referring to the pregnant mother's womb–is no longer associated with the idea of procreation here. The womb indeed undergoes displacement and is transferred onto, and designated as the stomach. The latter is not being viewed as the space of delivery here, but as the organ of ingestion, 'craving for the tart taste of mulberry' that 'sends Sardarji shouting for a servant to climb the tree shadowing the main drawing room' (192). The 'tongue' and the 'mouth' which are conjured up farther on the same page both spin the metaphor of the womb/stomach, underlining the idea of sensuality, which reaches a climax when the narrator adds that 'she even goes without her chunni occasionally, and her body seems unapologetically on fire' (192).

Sardarji also experiments with dismemberment, yet on an even more dramatic basis as he experiences split from within. His incapacity to deal with what he assumes to be the ontological superiority of the colonisers inevitably results in alienation. His *personage* is in many ways reminiscent of portraits of the 'Babu'– 'a subjudge, a clerk or overseer' that 'flounders while speaking, and stumbles and stutters', 'speaking in English'[22]– one regularly bumped into in early Indian English fiction. A canal engineer, he partakes of the colonial dismemberment of the country through the exploitation of its resources for the benefit of the British economy. Digging, separating, splitting and dividing the earth from within, Sardarji is just another agent of imperialism. And like the country, his very conscience seems to be dislocated. The haunting presence of a Doppelgänger, in other words, his *double*, Cunningham, conveys the depth of the identity crisis he is going through. A Punjabi accepting the values of English imperialism, he remains nonetheless concerned with his duties as a Sikh man, landlord and husband. He is in many ways akin to Rushdie's Aadam Aziz in *Midnight's Children*. Like him, he is a 'Europe-returned fellow', who seems to have cut the ties with his roots. His wife complains that she no longer understands the 'foreign languages' he 'fills' the 'heads' of the children with–'whatsitsname'![23] Just like Aadam Aziz, Sardarji, masters the colonisers' language. His own work under the leadership of 'his superior in the department, Mr. Timothy

---

22 'Bangali Babu', the song, can be read in S. Tharu and K. Lalita eds. *Women Writing in India*, I, 1991. It was written in 1880 by Mokshodayani Mukhopadhyaya, trans. Supriya Chaudhury, in Mehrotra, A.K. ed. *An Illustrated History of Indian Literature in English*, New Delhi: Permanent Black, Ravi Dayal Publisher, 2003, p.20.

23 Rushdie, Salman. *Midnight's Children*, Vintage, 1995, p.42.

Farquharson' (162) frequently brings the dummy lord out of him as we shall see later. His subjection to Cunningham reveals his subjection to Farquharson, who stands for the epitome of the country colonising. Cunningham is depicted as Sardarji's 'English-gentleman-inside' (159), demanding explanations for each and every deed the engineer performs. He is a kind of superego, interfering with Sardarji's freedom of action. It is little wonder that Cunningham should owe his name to Joseph Davey Cunningham, the 19th century historian of Sikhism. While the latter was the historian of a community born with a new religion, Sardarji's double is the historian of the Self here. One is the inventor of History, the other is the (re)creator of His (Sardarji's) story (His-story), i.e. the creator of the Self-subjected (i.e. the subject as opposed to the Self). Failing to learn what he wanted to take from the English in order to bring it back to India, Sardarji ends up *being* taught what he should *be* by the English. He is so to say displaced from his male position and re-placed into a female position Cunningham is even said to be *moving into* Sardarji, as he 'saddles Sardarji's mind', usurping his very freedom of thought within the frame of a somewhat intellectual form of rape. Cunningham embodies the imperialistic essence of the colonisers' discourse, revealing its ideological mechanisms, namely its systematic dismemberment of the Self. This is why Cunningham is able to 'edit paragraphs in Sardarji's mind before releasing them for utterance' (161). He has even devised a moral code of conduct, 'now that he has trained Sardarji on what is Done and Simply Not Done' (161). Alienation works on the basis of a reversal in the order of discourse: the colonisers' speech is displaced into the mind of the colonised, and that displacement leads to alienation, which is in turn revealed through language. Images conjuring up Sardarji's alienation on a metaphorical basis can be found in the sentence that establishes a parallel between the 'holy Ganga' and the 'River Thames' (160), and within the coinage referring to 'the British caste system', or in the picture of Sardarji standing 'Like an actor in a play', wearing a 'suit and pants' making him look like any Englishman, but for the 'turban' (161). Sardarji is even led to make a fool of himself when, having killed the boar Farquharson had failed to slaughter, he lets the Englishman claim his trophy. The image which depicts Sardarji's turban suddenly falling as it 'leaves his hair' while his 'topknot loosens' (231) is quite dramatic, in the sense that it provides readers with no less than an allegory of alienation, in keeping with Marx's definition from 1844:

> 'The alienation of the worker from his product means not only that his labour becomes an object, an external existence, but that it exists outside him, independently, as something alien to him, and that it becomes a power on its own confronting him; it means that the life he has conferred on the object confronts him as something hostile and alien.'[24]

In fact, Sardarji totally fails to be him-Self in front of the coloniser. According to Hegel's *The Phenomenology of Spirit*, it appears that Sardarji acts and *is acted* on (or made to act) as a slave, while Farquharson remains the master at all times:

> "L'individu qui n'a pas mis sa vie en jeu peut certes être reconnu comme *personne* ; mais il n'est pas parvenu à la vérité de cette reconnaissance, comme étant celle d'une

24 Marx, Karl. Economic and Philosophic Manuscripts of 1844, p. 70, quoted in Khair, Tabish. *Babu Fictions, Alienation in Contemporary Indian English Novels*, New Delhi: Oxford University Press, 2001, p. 24.

conscience de soi autonome. (….) chaque individu doit tendre à la mort de l'autre (…) son essence se présente à lui comme un autre, il est hors de lui-même ; il faut qu'il abolisse cet être hors de soi qui est le sien ; l'autre individu doit, est une conscience qui est (…) il faut qu'il contemple son être-autre comme pur être pour soi ou comme négation absolue." [25]

---

25 "He who has not yet put his life at stake can be recognised as a person; but he has not reached to the truth of that process of recognition as being that of an autonomous self-awareness. ...each person should strive for the death of the other (...) his essence is seen by him as an other's essence, it lies outside of himself. That other in that it is other-than-He has to abolish it; the other must be and is a conscience that is...He must look at his being-other as a being pour-soi or as an absolute negation."

III – The Body Remembered

Remembering the Novel

The very identity lies within the frame of dislocation and displacement. It is, so to say, *essentially* characterised by a sense of instability which accounts for its progression through flashbacks and prophetic speeches, as well as for the elements pertaining to dislocation and displacement.

Unstable chronology causes the narrative to be disrupted. Readers are hence made to make use of their memory, in order to remember the text properly. Memory, we have seen, is an abstract character in *What the Body Remembers*, but a character nonetheless. Taking on the shape of recurring syntactic patterns or didactic speech, Memory is depicted as a major element within the frame of the construction of the Self. The latter is rather viewed as a process, than as a fixed immutable entity. Present-time cannot be dissociated from the memory of what *was* or *is* in the characters' eyes. Time is time in 'this lifetime' (11), depending on other lives before. When Satya says she *remembers*, what she recalls is the 'suffering' (538) she actually 'endured', along with 'the waiting, the watching from the latent nothingness' she was caught in. It appears from this that is both looking back to the past, and looking forth to the present. As readers, we are encouraged to make use of our 'memories' to discover the signification of a certain number of events and consequently the logics governing the time schemes. The idea of a connection between memory/meaning is thus voiced by Satya's pointing out to us that: '*Each of us is changed by the roles we are given – the course of our change depends upon our pedigree and our past*' (297). Remembering the past involves remembering place and time. When conjuring up Roop's childhood, the narrator often colours it in euphoric tones. The memories of Pari Darvaza are bound to Gujri's delicious dishes: 'Closing her eyes, she can almost smell Gujri's special *makki rotis*. A path of fresh churned butter, white, gleaming, melting into the dark green of Gujri's spinach *saag*. She can almost feel the heat from the hot *makki rotis*, taste the tang of the mustard spinach ground for hours' (301). The Self exists on the condition that *It* remembers, i.e. provided *It* has borne the memory of the past within in order to literally figure out the present (and future). But figuring out subject-matter in *What the Body Remembers* also depends upon the use of memory we make as readers. Partition, we have seen, is gradually unveiled as being both the 'subject' and the structural matrix of the text. In fact, the experience of division in the microcosm – reaching its climax in Satya's usurpation of Roop's children – forecasts Partition in the macrocosm. Remembering and rearranging images of division we came across in the diegesis, will help us figure out the meaning of what happens when, towards the end of the book, Punjab undergoes the split the English decided they would achieve. Introducing the theme of Partition in *Midnight's Children*, Salman Rushdie resorted to an image of split as well: Saleem's mother shifting to Pakistan with her two children, and leaving her reluctant husband behind shows that the events occurring within the family cell reflect those which were happening in the country. Even more symbolic is the mutilation of Saleem's finger during a fight with his classmates, as the almost insignificant spilling of blood in the microcosm foretells future spilling of blood over the issue of Kashmir which, as we know, ranges among the symptoms of the body dismembered.[26] Back to *What the Body Remembers,* it seems that the progressive disintegration and break-up of the following couples, which are all structured around family bonds – Sardarji / Satya, Bachan Singh / his brother Shyam Chacha, Roop / Satya / Roop / her children – virtually heralds Partition as a process of dismemberment.[27] The image of the 'spout' that is 'affixed to the mouth of the underground stream scenting the core of Sardarji's haveli' (287) metaphorically designates the bonds between past / present, underground / surface, diegesis / History.

Baldwin's concern with memory is plain for all to see. From the point of view of reception, remembering the past is a *sine qua non* condition for re-membering the novel, i.e. for grasping meaning and binding the imagery of division to Partition. From a diegetic point of view, i.e. from the point of view of characters, remembering the past provides the narrator with the basis for a revision of History that might counter oppressive discourses emanating from the centre. As His-story, the past is regarded and conveyed from a colonising point of view, i.e. a masculine point of view. On the contrary, 'story' pertains to the private realm which is governed by female characters in the novel. Story is a prelude to

26 '...physical mutilations have a larger significance. They suggest the dismemberment of the nation. The partition with its tragic hacking of the nation, the increasing fragile and tenuous hold on Kashmir with the constant threat of a complete break away...all are indicators of a nation disintegrating.' (Ravi, P.S. *Modern Indian Fiction*, New Delhi, Prestige Books, 2003, pp. 84-85.

27 Sardarji rejected his barren and angry first wife, Shyam Chacha resented his brother Bachan Singh for having lapsed into Sikhism, while the bond between Roop / Satya is definitely broken as the first wife virtually steals Roop's daughter from her.

the re-membering and the telling of History. The female body is consequently viewed as a metaphoric battlefield, where several versions of History compete. The female body is meant – as we have seen earlier – to enact the His-story. But it has its own stories. Men strive to control females' bodies in order to define His-story.[28] In forbidding the women of the household to go to the Hindu temple, Bachan Singh wishes to prevent Revati Bhua from addressing Lakshmi instead of confiding in Vaheguru. He also intends to deter Roop and Madani from *listening* to Pandit Dinanath read the *Ramayana* (56). In this particular case, Hindu stories should be left behind to the benefit of the His-story of the ten Gurus. Bachan Singh acts in the same way as a coloniser, validating Baldwin's parallel between English (national) / Indian (domestic) colonisers. Strikingly enough, women's bodies are endowed with the capacity to resist His-story. Taking a closer look at the text, one soon realises that imperialistic versions of His-story – whether emanating from the English colonisers or from male characters having built up oppressive constructions of the feminine – are associated with the idea of immutability. Thus it is little wonder that the changes occurring in or on women's bodies are symptomatic of the females' revision of male His-story. Kusum's dismembered body on page 515 stands as an allegory of the impenetrability of history as opposed to His-story as it bears a 'message' which lies in the enigma of what happened to her really. Another image connoting the mystery of history – i.e. historical truth as having been denied by official His-story – is to be found in Bachan Singh's description of the Jallianwala Bagh massacre on page 61. He mentions 'the back walls' (62) of 'haveli compounds', resorting to the semantic field of confinement, insisting that the

28 Homi Bhaba often stresses the importance of the concept of 'fixity' in the ideological construction of otherness.

walls are 'very high'. Further, the evocation of a 'passage' counters the idea of opacity, suggesting the possibility and consequently viability of History (or story) as opposed to imperialistic His-story. It stands as a metaphor for the dialectics of story / history in *What the Body Remembers* where personal story is part of History. Further still, the image depicting the people in Jallianwala Bagh, 'some talking, laughing, playing cards, telling stories, some listening to speeches' (62) optimistically suggests the possible transmission of history through personal communication. But one could not fail to observe that the space of history-telling is essentially a masculine space: 'Roop struggles to keep her eyes open' (61). She is also said to be 'half listening' (62), offering 'no answers' (63) to her father's questions, while Revati Bhua snoozes and 'sighs' (65). Women seem to resent male His-story to the extent of ignoring it proper. But the father-and-son scene we lingered on infra shows that the core of imperialism is liable to displacement. The information he gives his own son about the events of Jallianwala Bagh shows that he attempts to counter the English colonisers' version of History: men and women are all liable to be subjected to His-story.

Sign and De-sign

The latter may be subjected to revision by the subject(ed), since what was once written can be erased. To put it in other terms, sign can be de-signed by the characters expressing desire for subversion(s) of History. A sign both material and spiritual, Roop's Urdu tattoo which (first introduced on page 70) is emblematic of some of the characters' capacity for subverting His-story. Though she expected the bangle seller to write her name 'in the Guru's script' (70) the man designed the tattoo as if 'he were writing it in Urdu', a language 'only Muslims use' (70) in an attempt to colonise Roop's (female) body. The writing on the girl's arm epitomises the power of language within the frame of religion. It literally underlines its power to define the Self or from an outsider's point of view an identity. But that power is eventually subverted as Roop fortunately escapes from death, because of the use she is going to make of the tattoo: Roop is ironically set free on the grounds that she is thought to be a Muslim (484). What was meant to be a sign – her tattooed name – is virtually designed to mean something else. However, Roop still remembers who, where and what she is as she reflects: '*Some men are not entitled to the truth*' (484). She is indeed confident that '*Vaheguru will understand*' (484) she had to design sign, i.e. to displace and dislocate the linguistic sign to design something and someone she was not for the sake of her family's survival.

The female body is the support upon which sign can be de-signed. It is the place where meaning intended becomes meaning subverted, where sign can be subverted into de-sign and where tradition can be re-membered proper. History almost systematically derives from the body, because the body actually bears testimony to the past. History cannot exist without the body, and conversely: "L'histoire, c'est en fin de compte l'histoire du lieu fantasmatique par excellence, c'est-à-dire le corps."[29] To Barthes, History is so to say ontologically derived from the experience of the Self *as* body proper. The bonds between History / Self as body are conveyed through the reversal of physical mechanisms within the body of some of the characters in *What the Body Remembers.* We all have in mind Amitav Ghosh's *The Shadow Lines,* where the author presents us with a central character whose sick stomach turns out to be a way of metaphorically personifying him. Using a capital letter to refer to his digestive pathology – 'Gastric' – the narrator suggests that Tridib's ways of dealing with History are specific. The strange ways of his stomach – normally performing the processes of ingestion and dismemberment – denote the character's dissatisfaction with the ways in which time is so to say arranged within the frame of His-story. Reversed physical mechanisms in *What the Body Remembers* are chiefly enacted by Roop: being partially deaf, she cannot cope with what is being asked or expected from her. The outside world has limited access to her. Partial (or partitioned) hearing causes the girl to be unable to always 'listen

29 'History is eventually the history of the fantastical locus par excellence, i.e. the body.' Barthes, Roland. *Leçon,* Paris: Editions du Seuil, p. 43.

and obey' as a recurring pattern wants it. Like her, though deliberately, Revati Bhua simply 'cups chubby hands over her ears' (56) as she does not wish to listen to Papaji. A little further the verb 'to listen' is mentioned before the narrator refers to 'good-good sweet-sweet obedient Sita', associating the activity of listening with the act of obeying.[30] The narrator even points out that Roop's defective ear embodies a sign of resistance. Like Satya's, her body's escaping from function challenges the values of the centre. Roop 'has mud in her other ear, too. Perhaps it's been there for a while, because she never heard Gujri or Revati Bhua say Huma was untouchable like Khanma' (78). 'Roop hears Huma's words with only one ear. Roop hears Huma's words, but she does not like what they say' (81). Her defective ear is endowed with the capacity to ignore hegemonic discourses concerning women, caste etc. Therefore, Roop is made free to re-member information from the outside world inside. But when one of her ears is disobedient, 'in Roop's good ear there are only Papaji's parting words, "Above all, give no trouble" (155). Another image of the defective body can be found in *Midnight's Children,* where the 'cracks' shaking Saleem's body[31] foretell those of Purusha's, the cosmic giant, i.e. 'the primeval male in a ritual Vedic sacrifice'.

30 Sita stands as the paradigm of woman as function. She has not questioned the gods' (men's) desire.

31 Mukherjee, Meenakshi. Rushdie's *Midnight's Children, A Book of Readings*, ed. Meenakshi Mukherjee, New Delhi:Pencraft International, 2003, p.159.

Selves Divided

Constructing the Self thus means deconstructing the Self, whose (dis)location (dis)places it from centre onto periphery. It appears from this that the Sikh community's current position in India is in many ways emblematic of the uncertain, and problematic location of the post-colonial Self as depicted in *What the Body Remembers*. Baldwin often insists on the paradoxical position of Sikhism and the Sikhs in India, lying between the Hindus on one side and the Muslims on the other. Listening to the cries emanating from tea stalls on page 89, Roop and Revati Bhua can hear that there is 'Hindu *chai*! Muslim *chai*!': ironically enough, there is no Sikh chai...Later, one observes that 'A *Hindu* purification ceremony' should probably not take place in 'a *Sikh* household' (80). The dislocation of Sikhism, i.e. its displacement from centre to periphery within the binary space constructed by religious imperialism epitomises the dislocation of the post-colonial Self. Though a woman like Sita, Roop is only mortal and not even allowed to believe in Ram or Sita because she is no longer a Hindu, but a Sikh' (201). Later in the text, the narrator adds that no 'water sprout' (89) has been 'provided (90) for the people who 'are neither Hindu nor Muslim' (399), and 'Sikhistan' does not exist, as Guru Nanak chose to 'walk his own path' (32). Taking up the metaphor of the path is quite revealing on the part of the author-cum-narrator as it suggests that there is both direction / uncertainty. In other words, the Guru (i.e. the Sikhs) know that they are on the way to location, but that location has not been defined.

The aesthetics governing speech in *What the Body Remembers* also lie within the frame of a dialectics of dislocation and re-membering: next to the technique of mixing, which was examined earlier lies the narrator's special ways of dealing with words by dividing them into parts, as a means of making more obvious their hybrid identity. Language is consequently relegated into the margins as it does not fit within regular linguistic boundaries. In sometimes resorting to neologisms, the narrator reveals the incapacity of so to say 'official' language to depict reality proper. The reference to a 'ghostman' on pages 37 and 91 reveals the narrator's / characters' comparison of English white men with 'ghosts', i.e. with a hyperbolic image of whiteness.

His language is referred as 'A deep voice', saying 'some words in a rough strange language' (37). A neologism, the noun 'ghostman' underlines the intrinsic capacity of language to unveil what has not been accounted for. Besides a few neologisms, one may come across coinages, like 'self-ness' on page 147. A compound of the keyword 'self' and of the suffix – 'ness', it is the translation of the word 'haumai', meaning self-consciousness. The use of a hyphen between the two compounds of the word proper, signals and signifies the hymen, insofar as we contemplate the metaphoric value of that membranous fold of tissue occluding the vaginal external orifice. The hyphen-hymen is the agent of re-membering. It reveals the presence of a sub-verting agent within the regulated language of the (male) centre. It is made clear here that 'Women treat the order of (male) domination in introducing chaotic syntactic structure, speaking in non-habitual ways, learning the alphabet of their bodies'[32] as Shormistha Panja observes, an alphabet that is figured within the hyphen-hymen. Next to 'self-ness' is the idea of 'unself-ness' (237), meaning to describe Roop's absolute reification of herself under 'Sardarji's weight...again' (237). The word 'give-ness' which is spelt with a hyphen as well – though the reason might be technical since the word might have been split in two for the sake of typographical needs (?)– is another attempt at re-membering women's 'truth'. It follows after the word 'for', which, added to the first part of the compound 'give' results in the verb 'forgive' which in turn suggests the re-placement of the noun 'for-give-ness' by the neologism 'give-ness'. The hymen, Derrida argues, 'merges with what it seems to be derived from...the vaginal partition, the fine, invisible veil, in front of the hystera, stands *between* the inside and the outside of a woman', a partition which locates woman (i.e. the paradigm of the post-colonial Self) neither in the present nor in the future but in between past / present.

Narrative voice also undergoes 'partition' taking on the shape of a mingling of languages and speeches within the frame of heteroglossia. The text indeed juxtaposes words coming from various Indian languages, like Urdu and Punjabi. It is little wonder that Bachan Singh's 'limited English' does not prevent him from writing 'Punjabi well', 'in both Persian and Gurmukhi scripts' (43). Juxtaposing Indian words and English translations, Baldwin achieves

32 Panja, Shormistha. 'Women and Literary Space', in Navati, U.M. and C. Kar, Prafulla ed. *Rethinking Indian English Literature*, New Delhi: Pencraft International, 2000, p. 95.

a visual illustration of Partition within speech. The narrator's reference to 'Sardarji's sister' Toshi, 'that *churail!* that witch!' (19) underlines the difference between two tongues, Hindi / English, and two categories, colonised / coloniser. Unlike Roop, 'Miss Barlow is deaf to this with both ears. If Roop speaks in Punjabi, her face blanks as if Roop were a jackdaw calling' (386): the boundaries between coloniser / colonised are made clear by the narrator's comparing Roop's language to that of an animal from the coloniser's point of view. But there is hope since both those female characters are women: this is why Roop dreams of a universal language that would be spoken and understood by both coloniser / colonised. Both personal pronouns 'I' and 'we' set on an equal footing in the sentence she coins inside her mind: *Use the words I have / maybe we can say...'* (386), voicing a tangible desire for shared understanding and communication.

Conclusion

What the Body Remembers exposes woman as the paradigmatic incarnation of the post-colonial subject, a self divided between past / present, tradition / modernity, here / there. Baldwin herself suggests the dislocation of the post-colonial self through her refusal to be ascribed a category in terms of authorship. She wants to be considered a diasporic writer, acknowledging her roots without renouncing her freedom as a creative artist. It is little wonder the novel ends up in "Indifferent Delhi" (485), the new capital where everything is to start again. In fact, the displacement and dislocation of boundaries in India has entailed a subsequent dislocation of identity which is best pictured by woman in the novel. The experience of Partition has compelled men to experiment with the space of the margins women have always been relegated into. *What the Body Remembers* retraces and mimics the traumatic experience of dislocation and displacement, an experience that is enacted by and within the diegesis as well as by the writing of the text itself. The author has indeed followed Virginia Woolf's advice to her readership and fellow writers: "adapt the body to the book" by turning it upside down in adapting the book to the body proper. Her work constitutes not only an enjoyable novel, but also a necessary compendium for those who wish to understand the origins and issues of contemporary feminism in India.

Appendix I

Documentary Glossary of Anglo-Indian and Indian languages, terms, book titles and names of authors and historical figures. Vade-mecum for the reader of *What the Body Remembers.*

Why a Documentary Glossary?

Shauna Singh Baldwin at no time wanted to add a glossary to her first novel *What the Body Remembers.* She did not want to relieve the reader of addressing the difficulty of coping with Indian words (over 350) and realities.

She had added however a map of pre-independence north-western India. Geographical knowledge was not expected from the reader but the work of looking for the Other was.

After I had read her novel several times and had started writing a kind of daybook for my own use, it occurred to me that this research, which tremendously enriched my view of this book could be useful to other readers. I took advantage of a short visit to Punjab the following year to get acquainted with its material culture and its landscapes. I saw the crops, the fields and the canals, the countryside and the bazaars, villages and havelis, I tasted the food and admired the beautifully crafted objects that were taken for granted by the characters in the novel. All these things, unknown to me at first, were as alien to many readers not familiar with Northern India or Pakistan.

I also added a few photographs shot during this invaluable tour with the hope to bring to the reader if not the savours and the fragrances mentioned in the novel, at least a visual idea of the characters' environment.

1. Amritsar, Golden Temple, Harmandir building, 1604, Punjab

2. Gurdwara, Bagian haveli, Punjab

3. Granthi and Guru Granth Sahib, Bagian, Punjab

4. Gurmurkhi, script, from Guru Granth Sahib, Haveli gurdwara

5. Offering Prayers at the Golden Temple, Harmandir SAHIB Amritsar, Punjab

6. Salwar-kameez, Punjabi traditional attire, Bagian, Punjab

7. Haveli, in Bagian, Punjab

8. Sarson field, Amritsar district, Punjab

9. Manji (charpoy), on the road to Wagah, Punjab

10. Village Sikhs

Kesh

Kara

11. Langar, Golden Temple, Amritsar

12. Punkha, collection

Glossary

Abbreviations
Ar: Arabic
H: Hindi
P: Persian
Pg: Portuguese
Pj: Punjabi
S: Sanskrit
Ur: Urdu

Aarti, H., religious ritual, adoration, here hymn composed by the first guru of Sikhism, sung during the evening prayer.

Abu, Ar., father

Achcha, H., yes, all right, well. *Achchaji*, yes, all right, with respect (*-ji*)

Agabarthi, H., thin incense stick.

Agniparishka, S./H., *agni*: fire. Self sacrifice of Sita, heroin of the most famous Indian epic (*Ramayana*), who walked and disappeared in the fire, who shamed her husband Rama who did not believe in her fidelity.

Ahista, Ur., slowly

Ahmadiyas, H., members of a sect founded in Pakistan ca 1889 by Mirza Ghulam Ahmad. Declared heretic in Muslim countries, the believers are now settled in northern India.

Ajjiber, Ur., weird, wonder.

Akali party, **Akali Dal**, H., Sikh movement founded in the 17th century to resist Mughal persecutions, restored as a party in the 1920s of the 20th century to defend the interests of the Sikhs in the Indian independence fight.

Akhbar, H./P., newspaper, news.

Akhand Paath, H., Sikh purification rite consisting of reading sacred texts of Sikhism.

Akhar, akhara, H., letter, character.

Ambi pattern, H., mango pattern.

Ami, Ur., mother.

Amla, H., *Embilica officinalis*, shrub of the myrobolan family, its gooseberry-like fruits are used to make chutneys. When powdered, amla is used in traditional medicine.

Amritsar,* a city in Punjab, centre of the Sikh faith, location of the *Harimandir*, Golden Temple, built by Arjun, the fifth Guru, in 1609 and restored by Maharajah Ranjit Singh (1801-1839).

Anjuman-i-Islamia Society, P., *anjuman*: assembly, meeting, society. Muslim Society.

Anna, H., Indian coin, one-sixteenth of a rupee, before the decimalisation (1957).

Apne aap, H., oneself, on one's own, without permission.

Ardaas, H., Sikh texts commemorating the martyrdom of the tenth Guru of the Sikhs, who refused to convert to Islam during the Mughal dynasty's rule.

Arjan tree, H., tree of Arjuna, *kumbuk*, *Terminalia arjuna*, an evergreen tree whose bark is used for dyeing, tanning and medical purposes.

Arya Samaj, H., *arya*: pur, *samaj*: society. Hindu reformist sect founded in 1875 by Dayanand Saraswati who called for the return to the original texts, an-iconic monotheism, equality of men and women, and uplift of the outcasts.

Aryan Hindu pantheon, S. a*rya*. Aryan tribes from Indo-European stock, said to have caused the collapse of the Indus valley civilisation, have settled in Iran and India, between 1700 and 1000 BCE. They brought their gods and their social organisation to the new land, where they overran local people and their pantheon.

Atma, atman, H., individual self, individual soul, the indestructible spirit of God.

Baba, H., term of respect or tender form of address between parents and children.

Babur of Samarkand, Babur (1483-1530), born in the Ferghana area (Uzbekistan), Zahir-ud-din Muhammad established the Mughal dynasty after his victory over Sultan Ibrahim Lodi in 1526.

Bachan, H., promise, commitment.

Baisakhi Festival, New Year according to the Hindu solar calendar.

Bandini dots, H., dots on a tie-dyed fabric, mainly from Rajasthan.

Baniya. H., Western India caste of merchants.

Bazaar, H./P., market, shopping area, in Indian towns.

Bebeji, Ur., mother.

Begum, H./P. a Muslim Indian queen or lady of high rank.

Begum Sahiba, respectful form of address to a lady.

Beti, H., daughter.

Bhainji, H., *Bhai*: brother/sister + *-ji* respectful address.

Bhang, H., *Cannabis Indica*, narcotic, whose dried leaves are smoked, chewed, or drunk.

Bhangra Pj., dancers, Punjabi dancers following a rhythmic folk music.

Bibi, Ur., (respectable) lady.

Bijar carpet, handwoven Kurdish carpet from Bijar in Western Iran. These stiff carpets have a double warp (chaîne), into which the weaver inserts a very tight weft (fil de trame).

Bindi, H., dot on the forehead of a Hindu wife. Forehead ornament.

Birada, H., dregs of tea, bad tea.

Biradari, H., brotherhood.

Bird-walla, Anglo-Indian, bird seller.

Bol, H., to speak, speech, word.

Bukvaas, **Bakvaas**, H., nonsense, absurd.

Bunyaan, H., Bra, breast cloth.

Burqa, H., from Ar., gown enveloping Muslim women in public, common in Pakistan and Afghanistan, not uncommon in India.

Chacha, H., paternal uncle.

Chachi, H., paternal uncle's wife.

Chador, H/P. I- large sheet used as shawl or mantle in Muslim India, two- cloth spread on Muslim tombs.

Chai, H., Indian tea (served with milk and sugar).

Chakra, S./H., one of the centres of spiritual power in the human body; wheel; a sharp-edged circular weapon of the Sikhs.

Chamar, H., a category of untouchable, outcast.

Chapli-kebab, H., flat kebab, flattened meat skewered and roasted.

Chaudhary, H., in northern India village headman or honorific title. Family name.

Chillum, Anglo-Indian, from H. *chilam*, from Ar., a part of the Indian pipe for smoking through water, which contains the tobacco and charcoal balls.

Chola, H., Indian millet, *Sorghum vulgare.*

Chota, H., (masc.) young, small.

Chota hazri, H. Light breakfast.

Choti-sardarni, H., (fem.), young Madam, second wife (in a Sikh context).

Choli, H., short-sleeved bodice, leaving the midriff bare. Worn with a sari or a long skirt.

Chun(n)a, H., lime, one of the ingredients of the betel chew.

Chunni,* H., long shawl worn by Punjabi women on their traditional costume of tunic and baggy trousers. It covers the head, the breast and shoulders for modesty.

Chura, H., low caste person, sweeper.

Churail, H., ghost of a woman who has died in childbirth, brings bad luck and disease.

Dacoit, from *dakait*, Anglo-Indian, member of a gang of armed robbers.

Dal, dhal, H., split pulse (lentils).

Dal, H., group, political party.

Deodar-wood, H./S., lit. tree of the gods: *Cedrus Deodara*, great cedar tree of the Himalayas.

Dhaap, Pj., slap.

Dhar-sound, H., sound of words.

Dhar(a)m, H./S., duty; obedience to the law; conduct fitting to one's essential nature.

Dharmaraj, H., *raj(a)* king; *dharm(a)* 'that which is established', respect of order and duty, corpus of principles by which all things exist. 'King of the netherworld'.

Dhoti, H., loincloth worn by men, wrapped around the body. The end passed between the legs and tucked at the waist.

Dihati, H., villager, peasant.

Dilruba, H., three or four-stringed instrument, with a long neck, played with a bow.

Diva, diya, H., terracotta oil lamp, with a small spout like indentation for the wick. Its shape dates back to the Indus Valley Civilisation.

Diwali, H./S., 'line of lights', Hindu festival of lights, occurring in October or November during the 'dark light of no moon'.

Djinn, H./Ar., an evil spirit, a ghost.

Doab, Ur., lit. 'two rivers', land between two rivers.

Draupadi, wife of the five Pandava brothers in the great Indian epic poem *Mahabharat(a)*.

Durbar, darbar, H./P., royal audience, the hall of royal audience.

Dussehra, Dassehra, H., lit. Tenth Day, Hindu festival commemorating Rama's prayer to the goddess Durga who was sleeping for nine days. The tenth day she woke up and gave Rama the victory over his enemy giant Ravana, King of Lanka and abductor of Sita.

Egg-bhurji, H., scrambled eggs with chopped onions.

Ekka, H., a one horse Indian carriage.

Fatwa, H./Ar., judicial decision made by a Muslim doctor of the law.

Firman, H./P., imperial order.

Gandhi, Mohandas Karamchand (1869-1948), known as Mahatma Gandhi, leader of India's struggle for independence. A lawyer, he developed the theory of *ahimsa*, non-violence, and preached for secularism. Although he pleaded for the harmonious coexistence of different castes, classes and religious communities, he was unable to prevent the Partition of British India and the founding of a separate Muslim state wanted by Mohammed Ali Jinnah and the Muslim League.

Ganga, S., Indian goddess personified in the River Ganges, sacred stream of India.

Gautama Buddha, (ca 550 – ca 480 BCE) founder of Buddhism, a reaction against the power of the Brahmins. Born to a Kshatriya family of northern Bihar, the Sakya led a princely life until, after four dramatic encounters with a poor, a sick, a dead man and an ascetic, he turned to traditional Hindu ascetism. After he realised the inanity of ascetism, he created his own philosophy, experienced the *bodhi*, illumination, and devoted the rest of his life to preaching his moral, egalitarian way to liberation. He is known as the Buddha, one who reached the *bodhi*, and as Sakyamuni, the monk of the Sakya.

Ghalib, Mirza Asadullah Khan, (1797-1869) famous *ghazal* writer in Urdu and Persian.

Ghazal, H./Ur., fr. P./Ar., originally a love poem addressed to a doe-eyed (or gazelle-eyed) beauty. One of the main forms of north Indian poetry, sung with a musical accompaniment of *tabla* drums and a string instrument.

Git-mit, a kind of onomatopeia used by the character of Satya, imitating the sound of the English language.

Gobar, H., cow dung.

Godown, Anglo-Indian, a stocking area, an underground reserve.

Grand Trunk Road, Anglo-Indian, national highway, called today Sher Shah Marg, linking most great cities of northern India.

Granthi,* H., Sikh dignitary, guardian and reader of the Sikh holy text in a temple. Not a cleric, he is a functionary appointed by his community.

Gulmohar tree, H., *Delonix regia*, flamboyant, flame-tree.

Gur(u)bani, Gurvani., H, lit. the words of the *Guru* (God), from the *Guru Granth Sahib.*

Gur(u)dwara,* H., lit. house of the Guru, a Sikh temple.

Gurkha, Anglo-Indian, British soldiers from a Nepalese tribe. General Dyer's soldiers at Jallianwala Bagh in Amritsar in 1919 were Gurkhas.

Gurpurb, H., lit. Guru's day, anniversary of the birth or the death of a Sikh Guru.

Guru, H., a spiritual teacher, the head of a religious sect. In a Sikh context, also God.

Gur(u)mukhi,* H., lit. 'from the mouth of God'. The script (a variant of the *Devanagari* script of Sanskrit) in which the texts of Sikhism and the modern Punjabi language are written.

Guru Granth Sahib,* H., holy book of the Sikh religion, also called Adi Granth. Written in Punjabi and *Gurmukhi* script, it is a collection of hymns in praise of God.

Guru Tegh Bahadur, (1621-1675), ninth Sikh Guru, executed in Delhi on Mughal Emperor Aurangzeb's order (1618-1707).

Hakim, Ur./P., fr. Ar., philosopher, medical doctor, doctor of the law.

Halwai, H., *Halwa* seller, a sweet made of milk, sugar, almond paste and clarified butter (*ghee*).

Hanji, Pj., yes, well.

Hanuman, a deity and a character in the epic *Ramayana*. The Divine Monkey, who at the head of his army helped exiled King Rama to recover his wife and position.

Harappa, eponymous site of the Harappan or Indus civilisation (2500-1700 BCE), in today's Pakistan. This pre–Aryan site bears testimony to the high cultural and technical level reached during the Bronze Age by the first inhabitants of India, whose culture was overrun by the Aryan invaders, and whose gods became Indian lesser gods.

Haumai, H., self-ness, I-ness, self-centred pride.

Haveli, H., big house, fortified residence, palace.

Henna, Ur., fr. Ar. *heena, Lawsonia,* shrub whose powdered dried leaves are used to dye the hair or draw body designs for ritual purposes and weddings.

Hindu, follower of the Hindu religion. Hinduism has three main gods: Brahma, Vishnu and Shiva. The founding texts are the *Vedas* (S. radical *vid-*, to see), in four collections: the *Rig Veda* (solemn recitation) written ca 1500-900 BCE, the *Sama Veda* (liturgical hymns), the *Yajur Veda* (sacrificial incantations) and the *Atharva Veda* (incantations and magic formulas). The priests are the Brahmins, the highest of the four Indian castes (*varnas*). Great epics of Hinduism are the *Mahabharata* and the *Ramayana*.

Huzoor, H., fr. Ar. *Huzur,* an important person or his personal attendant.

Ik mint, H., one minute.

Ik(k)at, Indonesian word, faded pattern on textiles, obtained by the tie-dye technique.

Imli, H., fr. S. *amlika, Tamarindus indica,* fruit of the tamarind tree, used as medicine and in cookery.

Indus River, fr. S. Sindhu, river, cradle of the Indus or Harappan civilisation.

Inquilab, inqilab, Ur./P., fr. Ar. Revolution.

Inqilab zindabad, Long Live the Revolution ! in Persian. What the Pakistanis shout at Wagah (post on the boarder between Amritsar and Lahore).

Ismaili, Ismaili Muslims, followers of a minor Shia sect, whose spiritual leader is the Aga Khan. They are mainly living in India, Pakistan, Iran, Africa and Syria.

Iz(z)at, Ur., honour, good reputation, self-respect.

Jag(h)ir, H./P., a hereditary assignment of land and of its rent from a king or a government's share of a district revenue to a person.

Jag(h)iri hunger, H., avidity.

Jag(h)irdar, H/P., holder of a *jaghir*, who collects revenue from a tract of land, for state purposes or personal support.

Jai Hind, H., 'long live India!'

Jalal-ud-din-Rumi (1207-1273), great poet of love and *Sufi* thinker, in the Persian language.

Jallianwala Bagh, a public garden in Amritsar, accessible by a narrow corridor and surrounded by buildings, where on April 13, 1919, General Dyer ordered his Gurkhas to shoot the crowd of Indian demonstrators (20 per cent of Sikhs). They had gathered to protest against the newly established British policy of repressing subversive (hence nationalist) activities assimilated to 'activity by an external enemy'.

Jamahwar* shawl, H./P.,long piece of fabric with complex decorative woven motifs, with or without a border.

Jamun tree, H., *Eugenia jambolana*, the Java plum tree, tall evergreen tree.

Janam-sakhi, commemorative songs on Guru Nanak's life, written in the second half of the 17th century.

Japji, H., Sikh morning prayer.

Jatha, Pj., a group of citizens.

Jarokha-window, H., stone screen, oriel window, from which one can see without being seen.

Jelsy, corruption or jealousy.

Jezail, jazail, H/P., long, heavy Afghan musket.

Jheel, H., a pool or small stagnant lake left after the rains.

Jeevan, H., life, a first name.

Jhelum, Jhelam River, H., one of the five tributaries of the Indus River, which gave its name to the Punjab.

Jinnah, Mohammed Ali (1876-1948), Muslim lawyer born to a merchant family, educated in law at Lincoln's Inn in London. Nationalist and leader of the Indian Muslim League. He obtained from the colonial power in 1947 the Partition of British India into the Republic of India and Pakistan, the Land of the Pure, of which he became the first Governor General.

Juma, P., Muslim Friday prayers.

Juldee, H., fast, quick.

Jyotshi, H., Astrologer.

Kaan malliya, Pj., ear cleaner.

Kabbadi, Tamil/H., chasing game between two teams of nine.

Kachcha, H./Pj., short underpants worn by the Sikh men.

Kafir, H., fr Ar., non-believer, infidel.

Kakar, H., *Muntjak* deer, barking deer.

Kakeyi, in the *Ramayana*, Rama's stepmother and enemy.

Kakkar,* H., obligation, the five *kakkars* of the Sikhs are: to wear a *kara*, bracelet, to sport *kesh*, long hair and beard, to wear *kachcha*, short pants, to carry a *kirpan*, sword, and a *kanga*, comb. Originally the turban is not compulsory.

Kaliyug, H., the current era, goddess Kali's, fierce aspect of Parvati (Durga), Shiva's spouse.

Kameez, H./P./Ar., long shirt worn with baggy trousers in Afghanistan, India, Pakistan.

Kantha,* H., necklace, close to the neck.

Kara,* H./Pj., steel bracelet worn by Sikh men and women. One of the five obligations.

Karakuli-cap, cap made of the skin of a Karakul baby lamb or foetus, originally from Western Iran. Better known as Astrakhan cap.

Karma (n), S./H., action, fate. The sum of a person's actions in one of his existences determines his fate during the next one. Only the attainment of perfection permits the liberation : the merging of the individual with god Brahma.

Kava tea, H., cardamom tea, popular in Kashmir.

Kebab, H./Ar., roasted skewered pieces of meat.

Kerman, design, motif typical on carpet from Kirman, a city in south-eastern Iran.

Kes(h), * H., one of the Sikh's obligations, not to cut hair and beard.

Keshgundun, H./Pj., Sikh ceremony, when a boy ties his first turban.

Khana, H., food, dinner.

Khand, H., post-mortem stage of awareness when the dead awaits liberation or reincarnation, in the Sikh religion.

Kheer, H., pudding.

Khichri, H., mixture of rice and skinned and broken lentils, cooked at a low temperature for a long time.

Khilafat, H./Ar., Muslim anti-British movement in India after 1920.

Khuda hafiz, H./P., Muslim greeting, goodbye.

Kikar tree,* H., *Acacia Arabica*, the tree which produces Arabic gum (pharm.)

Kikli, a game, two children join hands and spin.

Kirat, Pj., hard work.

Kirtan Sohila, H./Pj., extract of the *Guru Granth Sahib*, sung as evening prayer and prayer for the dead.

Kismet, kismat, H./Urdu/ Turkish., the destiny of a person, his lot.

Kohinoor, P., mountain of light, big diamond (over 100 crt) which passed into the hands of the Mughal Emperor Shah Jahan, reached Sikh Maharajah Ranjit Singh, then was taken by the British and was set in the middle of Queen Elizabeth's crown in 1937.

Kolhapuri sandals, thong-like leather sandals from Kolhapur, in Western India.

Koran, Quran, Ar., the sacred book of Islam, God's words revealed to Muhammad.

Kshatriya, S., second caste (warriors, kings) in the Indian society, above the Vaishya, merchants and the Sudras, servants.

Kundalini-snake, S., coiled snake.

Kursi, H., chair.

Kuti, H., bitch.

Lambardar, H., village head or a peasant registered on the tax collector's roll.

Langar,* Pj., community kitchen within a Sikh temple.

Lavaan, Pj., circumambulations around the *Guru Granth Sahib* as part of a marriage ceremony.

Lehnga,* H., long skirt worn in Rajasthan, and in northern India, with a short blouse and a long head veil (*chunni*).

Log, lok, H., people.

Lohri, H., midwinter festival (January13) popular in Punjab. Celebration of fire, *Agni* and sun, *Surya*.

Loo wind, H., fr. S. *ulka*, flame, a hot wind laden with dust, in Punjab and Bihar.

Lori rhymes, H./Pj. Lullaby.

Mahabharat(a), one of the two great epics of Indian literature in Sanskrit. Relates the exploits of the five Pandava brothers and their common wife Draupadi, supported by the Divine Krishna in their struggle against their evil cousins the Kauravas.

Mahavira Jain, (born in Bihar ca 599 BCE). A Kshatriya, founder of reformist religious sect Jainism, in reaction to the power of the Brahmins. Strict vegetarianism and importance of monastic life.

Maharaja Ranjit Singh (1780-1839), founder (1799) of the Sikh Kingdom of Punjab, got rid of the Afghans in Punjab, but his Sikh state was overrun by the British in 1843. Known as the Lion of Punjab, he invited European experts, civil and military, to his court. Several French generals served him.

Mahmud of Ghazni (971-1030), founder of the first Muslim Afghan dynasty (Ghaznavid).

Mahout, mohaut, H., a driver and attendant to an elephant.

Makki roti, H., typical Punjabi flat bread, made of corn flour.

Mali, H., a gardener, he also makes garlands and flower arrangements.

Mal(l)ika (Victoria), Ar./P., a princess, here Queen Victoria.

Mangal, H./S., the Mangal star: Mars, auspiciousness. Mangalsutra: gold pendant worn by Hindu wives for good luck.

Manji, * Pj., for Hindi *charpoy*, four-footed light bed with a mattress of woven string,

Matlab, **mutlub**, H. fr. Ar., question, wish, intention.

Maulvi, H. fr. Ar., a Muslim judge or a learned man in Arabic or Persian.

Maund, Pj., mound, a heap.

Mehmaan, H./P., stranger, guest.

Mehnu, H., to me. **Mehnu piara**, dear to me.

Mia, **Mian**,Ur., husband, Sir.

Milavat, Pj., mixture.

Milni ceremony, H., first meeting of the families of bride and groom before the wedding, after the arrangements have been made. Hindu as well as Sikh.

Miltry duty, corruption of military duty.

Mint-skint, corruption of minute, second.

Mir Taqi Mir, 18th century poet, author of famous *ghazals* in Urdu.

Mohalla, H./Ur., fr. Ar., a neighbourhood, an area.

Mo(h)enjodaro, in Pakistani Punjab, the site of a great city of the Indus civilisation.

Mohur, H./P., Indian gold coin, used from the 16th century to the colonial period.

Muezzin, Ar., the man (lay) who calls the believers to the prayer, from the minaret of a mosque. Islam does not have priests.

Mughal, **Moghul**, Ur./P., from Mongol. Central Asian tribes of Mongolian origin who conquered India where they founded an empire and a dynasty of seventeen rulers. (16th - 18th century.)

Muhammad (ca 570-632), born in Mecca, founder of Islam, revealed to him by the words of God, recorded in the Koran. Islam is one of the three Western monotheisms.

Muhammad Iqbal (1877-1938), famous Punjabi poet in Persian and Urdu. A lawyer and philosopher educated at Cambridge, he fought for an independent Muslim state and the partition of India.

Mukaish* embroidered, Hindi, small pieces of gold or silver, fixed on a fabric.

Mukhtiar, Ur., house manager.

Mullah, H. fr. Ar., a learned man, a teacher who reads from the Koran.

Mulligatawny soup, Anglo-Indian fr. Tamil, curry soup.

Muslim League, Muslim movement founded in 1906. In 1940 under the leadership of Jinnah, fought for an independent Muslim state, Land of the Pure, Pakistan.

Munshi, H., secretary, writer.

Mynah, H., the Indian talking starling (étourneau).

Nahinji, H., *nahin* negation + -ji suffixe de politesse.

Namaaz, H./ P., Muslim prayers.

Namaste, Hindu greeting.

Namdhari Sikh, H., vegetarian, puritanical sect of Sikhism, whose followers wear a white turban flat on the forehead.

Nanak, Guru Nanak (1469-1539), founder of Sikhism, born in Lahore (Pakistan), active in Punjab. A *Sant* in the north Indian Bhakti tradition, he preached a strict an-iconic monotheism. First author of the Sikh Holy Book, a collection of hymns in praise of God, the Guru Granth Sahib. Love of God (a-morphic, without attributes), inanity of the caste system, hard work, sharing of resources with the neighbours, fitness of the body, are the first steps towards liberation. After him nine gurus were at the head of the Sikh religion, they completed his teaching and writing, and added to the Guru Granth Sahib.

Nankana Sahib, Guru Nanak's birthplace, in Lahore.

Navrati, H., in Hinduism, the nine nights devoted to goddess Durga, two periods per year: in April before Rama's birthday, the second one before Dussehra, celebrating Rama's victory over Ravana.

Nawaab, nabob, H./Ar., Muslim governor or aristocrat.

Neem,* H., Margosa tree, *Azadirachia indica,* sacred for Hindus, its leaves and bark are used in traditional medicine. Neem twigs are a natural toothbrush.

Nihang Sikh, H., member of a military order founded in the 17th century by Guru Hargobind Singh. Known for their bravery, they wear long blue and orange tunics, and high blue turbans, in which they keep steel throwing quoits.

Office-walla, H., Anglo-Indian, office boy.

Paan,* H., betel chew, made of a betel (of the black pepper family) leave wrapping, a mix of spices *kattha* paste, cardamom with lime paste and tobacco.

Paandaan,* H., betel chew container.

Paap, H., duty of a man of responsibility towards his family members and clients.

Pakora, H., vegetable fritter.

Palloo,* H., the upper end of the sari, passing over the left shoulder and hanging on a lady's back.

Pandit, pundit, S./H., a learned man, in Sanskrit, philosophy, religion and Hindu law. Any learned expert.

Pani, H., water.

Parshaad, prasad, Pj./H., a delicacy, made of flour or semolina with *ghee* and sugar, offered and shared. Visitors, Sikh and non-Sikh, receive a portion before leaving a *gurdwara.*

Parsi, lit. Persian, Iranian. Follower of the Zoroastrian religion. With the arrival of Islam in the 7th and 8th centuries, Zoroastrians fled from Persia and settled in India, where their descendants have a highly educated, prosperous community. With unmarried specialised clerics, the Parsis worship fire.

Pathan Muslims, Pashto-speaking Muslim tribes on both sides of the Afghan border.

Patwari, H., village headman, in charge of land and/or civil status registry.

Pauri, H., stanza of a *var,* ode. An Adi Granth consisting of *pauris* with preceding *shaloks.*, short couplets.

Peher, H., a fraction.

Persian wheels, noria, irrigation device.

Peshawari kurta-salwar, Punjabi costume, baggy trousers and tunic, in the style of Peshawar.

Peththa, H., cubes of pumpkin or papaya, marinated in limestone and water, and crystallised in sugar.

Phulkari–embroidered,* Pj./H., lit. flower work. Typical Punjabi embroidery of silk thread (mainly red, orange) on a home-woven dull red-brown background. Such shawls or bed covers are part of a girl's dowry and of a family's heirloom.

Piara, H., dear.

Pinni sweets, Pj., made of semolina, almonds, pistachios, cooked in pure ghee.

Pippal, **peepal**,* H., *Ficus religiosa*, sacred fig tree. Called *Bodhi* tree in a Buddhist context (the Buddha experienced illumination under a *pipal* tree).

Pir, H./P., Muslim saint or holy man.

Piri, H., stool.

Poochal, Pj., tail.

Pothwari, from the Pothwar plateau, between the Indus and Jhelam rivers.

Prakrit, H., fr. S *prakrta*, natural, vulgar, op. *sanskrta*, refined, prepared. Vernacular Indian languages evolved from Sanskrit and the first Indo-Aryan languages.

Pukkha, Pj., **punkha**, **pankha**,* Hindi and English, a wing-shaped hand fan made of palm leaf or swinging fan made of cloth and worked by a rope pulled by a servant.

Pukkhawala, Pj., **punkhawallah**, Hindi, Anglo-Indian, the servant in charge of the fan.

Punjab, H., *panj*, five; *ab*, river. Area of the Indus River basin and its five tributaries: Chenab, Ravi, Sutlej (Gr. Zaradros), Beas (Gr. Hyphasis) and Jhelam (Gr. Hydaspes)

Purdah, **pardah**, H./P., curtain, veil, state of seclusion of women in northern India.

Puri, H., fried thin wheat bread.

Q(u)aid-e-Azam, H./Ar., great leader, father of the nation, appellation of Jinnah, father of the Pakistan state.

Qaw(w)al, H./P., North-Indian vocal music, accompanied by a musical instrument, most often one or several harmoniums. *Quawwali* singers are professional singers.

Q(u)om, H./Ar., community, social group.

Rabab, Rebab,* H./Ar., three or four-stringed instrument, played with a bow.

Raja, S., H. *raj*, king, lord cf. Latin *rex, regis.*

Ramayan(a), fr. S. *Ramayana, The Romance of Ram(a)*. One of the great epic poems of India, written in Sanskrit by Valmiki, not before 300 BCE. After an intrigue put up by his stepmother, Prince Ram(a) leaves his father's court to live in the forest with his brother Lakshman(a) and his wife Sita. She gets abducted by giant evil King Ravan(a) of Lanka. With the help of god Krishna, Ram(a) recovers her but doesn't believe she has remained faithful. In a self-justifying reprisal, Sita commits suicide walking in a fire.

Ramazan, H./Ar., ninth lunar month, Muslim lent, Ramadan.

Ram-Lila, H., the next day after the Dussehra festival.

Rakhri, rakhi, H., string bracelet acting as a protection when offered a 'brother' at the full moon festival after the mosoon.

Rani, ranee, H. fr. S. *rajni* (cf. Lat. *regina*), a *raja*'s wife. Title.

Ratti, H., red, seed of a creeper, *Abrus pecatorius,* used as a weight by goldsmiths.

Rehraas, H., *Rahiras* in Pj., evening prayers at the closure of the Guru Granth Sahib for the night.

Rice pilau, H./P., rice boiled with meat, spices and raisins.

Rishta, H., a relation, an alliance.

Roop, S. *rupa*, form, here used as a proper name.

Saag, H., pureed green vegetable, *palak ka saag,* spinach *saag, sarson* ka saag,* mustard *saag* are Punjabi favourites.

Safa-cloth, H., turban.

Sahadjadhari, H., Shorn Sikh, who doesn't respect the obligation of *kesh* (long hair and beard) nor *kangha* (wear a comb in his hair).

Sahib, Saab, H./Ur., fr. Ar., a lord, form of respect.

Sahukar, H., moneylender, 'banker'.

Salaam, Ar./H., peace, Muslim greeting.

Salma-sitara, H., a gold or silver sequin work on a fabric (on *chunni, lehnga*).

Salver, H., a large tray.

Salwar, H./Ur., fr. Ar. Saroual, baggy pants.

Salwar-kameez,* H./Pj., traditional Punjabi dress worn by men and women.

Samadhi, S., the state of union with creation which a perfected yogi is said to pass at his apparent death. Hence site of the burial of a holy man.

Sant, H./Pj., title of wandering ascetics of the *Bhakti* tradition of Hinduism and of Sikhism. The *Sant* tradition is a devotional school of north India which stresses the need for inner religion.

Sardar, Ur./P., a military leader; a title of respect. *Sardarji*, a proper form of address to a Sikh. Fem. *Sardarni*.

Sat Sri Akal, H./Pj., Sikh greeting between men of the same social status.

Satya, S., truth, here used as a character's name.

Saukan, Pj., co-spouse.

Savayan, savaiyan, H., vermicelli, noodles boiled in milk or *ghee* with sugar, honey and spices, popular in north-eastern India.

Sepoy, sepahi, H./P., horseman, a soldier in the British forces. They rebelled in 1857.

Shaandaar, Pj., grand.

Shabad, Ur., Sikh hymn praising God, from the Guru Granth Sahib.

Shakti, S./H., all pervading divine energy, incarnated in the Mother Goddess Shakti, one of the aspects of Shiva's consort Devi, Uma, Parvati, Durga, Tara.

Shairi, Ur., Urdu sung poetry practised in a group of poets.

Shamiana, H., tent.

Shamla-fan, Anglo-Indian, part of a ceremonial turban, pleated like a fan.

Shahtoosh, H., ring shawl, light shawl woven with the hair of the Tibetan antelope, an endangered species. Making, trading of *shahtoosh* is prohibited.

Sheikh, H./Ar., in India, Hindu convert to Islam.

Sher, H., tiger.

Sher Shah, (1486-1545), Afghan invader and emperor of northern India (1540-1545). Sher Shah Marg, Indian name of the Great Trunk Road.

Shervani, H., traditional long coat worn by Indian men, buttoned up to the neck.

Sheesh mahal,* H./P., a hall or suite of rooms lined with small mirrors (they reflect the light of candles or lamps) in palaces and havelis.

Shia, Ar., one of the two great Muslim sects. For Shias Prophet Muhammad's cousin-cum-son-in-law and descent are his legitimate successors to the Caliphate. Mainly present in Iran, Iraq and India.

Shikar, H., hunt.

Shisham-wood, H., *Dalbergia Sissoo*, Indian wood, used in architecture, cabinet making and shipbuilding.

Shuddhi, H., pure, unadulterated.

Shukriya, H., thank you.

Shunya, S., zero.

Siapa, H., Hindu purification ceremony, ritual.

Sikh, H., a follower of the Sikh religion. Sikhism is a strict monotheism, opposed to the worship of icons and rejecting the caste system. Its main temple is the Gold Temple in Amritsar. It was founded in Punjab in the 16th century by Guru Nanak (1469-1539), who had nine successors, the last one, Guru Gobind Singh (1666-1708), founded a military fraternity, the Khalsa, to resist Mughal persecutions.

Simla-mirch peppers, H., large fleshy capsicum.

Sita, one of the main characters in the *Ramayana*, Rama's abducted faithful wife.

Sitala, S., a name of Mother goddess Shakti, as goddess of smallpox.

Sowar, H./P., horseman, mounted trooper.

Subehdar, H., local commandant or chief officer.

Sufi, H./Ur./P./Ar., follower of a Muslim mystic sect, in Turkey, Iran and the Indian continent. Sufism borrowed from Neo-Platonism and, in India, to Indian philosophy and religion. In Punjab, the doctrines of two *sants*, Kabir (1440-1518), Hindi poet and religious preacher, and Nanak (1469-1539), his disciple and founder of Sikhism, bear testimony to the interaction of Indian Sufism and Hinduism.

Sukhmani, H., a prayer 'of peace and happiness'.

Sunni, Ar. One of the great Muslim sects, orthodox, they recognise the four first Caliphs as Muhammad's legitimate successors.

Surma(h)-blackened eye, H/P., kohl, antimony sulphate, a black powder used to darken eyelids and eyebrows.

Suryanamaskar, S., Yoga posture, 'Greeting the sun'.

Suttee, sati, H./S., a self-immolated widow on the funeral pyre of her husband; the act of self-immolation of a widow.

Tachey case, Punjabi Anglo-Indian. Bag, case.

Taj Mahal, P./Ar. Marble mausoleum, erected in Agra (1632-1642) by fifth Mughal Emperor Shah Jahan (1592-1666) in memory of his favourite wife Begum Mumtaz Mahal, who had died in childbirth.

Tandav dance, God Shiva's fierce dance of destruction and re-creation of the universe.

Tap(p)as, H./S., poems by ascetics, about austere devotion. As a means of passive resistance to the British rule.

Tara Singh (1885-1967), born Hindu in Rawalpindi, he converted to Sikhism as a student and within the Akali Dal Party took up the Sikh cause. He fought for a separate state with Sikhism as official religion and Punjabi as official language. Nehru refused in the name of secularism in 1961. Although the state of Punjab was cut out in northern India in 1967, though most of its inhabitants are Sikhs, it is not the Sikhistan nor the Khalistan that Sikh activists yearned for.

Teacher-ni, Anglo-Indian, respectful form of address for a female teacher.

Thal, thali, H., plate on which a complete Indian meal of several dishes is served.

Thatha-cloth, H., net.

Tiffin-carrier, Anglo-Indian, a tiffin is a light lunch carried in several containers superimposed, to be brought from home to the workplace by an employee.

Tikka, tika, tilka, tilak, H., earth or pigment mark on a man or a woman's forehead. Mark of blessing at a Hindu ceremony. (not to be mistaken for the *bindi*).

Toady-bac(c)ha, Anglo-Indian, sycophant, bootlicker.

Tonga, tanga, H., light two-wheeled horse-drawn vehicle for four passengers.

Topee, topi, Anglo-Indian fr. Pg. Hat. In India the *pith-helmet*, sun-helmet.

Tulsi,* H., holy basil of Hinduism, *Ocymum sanctus*, worshipped as a symbol of Goddess *Tulsi Mata*. As sacred as Ganges water, it sanctifies food and is used in medicine.

Ujjai, H. fr. *unchi*, with effort. Ujjai-breathing, breathing with effort, to diminish the pain of giving birth.

Urdu, Indo-European language, close to Hindi, spoken in north-western India (today's Pakistan), written in Arabic characters. It borrows vocabulary from Persian and Arabic, more than Hindi which relies preferably on Sanskrit. Amateurs of classical poetry and music, in India as well as in Pakistan, consider Urdu as the literary language *par excellence*.

Uttar, attar, P./H., perfume, essence. *Attar* of roses, *attar ghul*, essence of roses.

Vaheguru, H., in Sikhism a term for God, *wah* Hindi exclamation of excellence.

Vaqt, H., a given period of time.

Veto-sheeto, H., derisive term for a document with the Viceroy's veto.

Virk, H., silver, as on a sweet.

Zamana, H./P., age, era, time.

Zamindar, H./P., landowner and tax collector.

Zanana, zenana, H/P., harem, women's quarter.

Zarda, H., one of the spices in a betel chew.

Zevar, H., gold.

Zindabad, P., life

Zohr, H/P., Muslim prayer.

Appendix II

Bibliography

Primary Sources

Singh, Baldwin, Shauna. *What the Body Remembers,* New Delhi: Nan Talese/Doubleday, 1999, HarperCollins Publishers India, 2000.

Singh, Baldwin, Shauna. *English Lessons and Other Stories,* Fredericton, New Brunswick: 1996, 1999.

Singh, Khushwant. *Train to Pakistan,* New Delhi: Permanent Black, 1988.

Ghosh, Amitav. *The Shadow Lines,* first published New Delhi: Ravi Dayal, 1988, reprint 1998.

Kapur, Manju. *Difficult Daughters,* London: Faber and Faber, 1988, reprint New Delhi: Penguin Books India, 2002.

Roy, Arundhati. *The God of Small Things,* New Delhi: IndiaInk, 1997, reprint New Delhi: Penguin Books India, 2002.

Rushdie, Salman. *Midnight's Children,* first published London: Jonathan Cape Ltd. 1981, reprint London: Vintage, 1995.

Kipling, Rudyard. *Kim,* first published London: 1901, reprint London: Penguin Books, 1989.

Critical Sources

Internet

Bold Type. Essay by Shauna Singh Baldwin:
www.randomhouse.com/boldtype/1199/badlwin/essay/html

Mary Soderstrom: Shauna Singh Baldwin, From the Punjab to Montreal and Back Again:
www.geocities.com/marysoderstrom/baldwin/html

Shauna Singh Baldwin-Interview re *What the Body Remembers* January 2000:
www.umiacs.umd.edu/users/sawweb/sawnet/books/SSBBordersInterview/html

Quill and Quire:
www.quillandquire.com/authors/profile.cfm?article_id=1542

The Sikh Times – Book Reviews –A Partition of the Truth:
www.sikhtimes.com/books_092599a.html

Anjana Basu: A Self Divided
www.sawf.org/newedit/edit03182002/bookreview.asp
www.emory.edu/ENGLISH/Bahri/Pub.html

Dictionaries Consulted for the Making of the Glossary

- Hankin, Nigel. *Hanklyn-Janklin, a Stranger's Rumble-Tumble Guide to Some Words, Customs and Quiddities Indian and Indo-British*, New Delhi: Banyan Books, 1994, New Delhi: India Research Press, 2003.

- Lewis, Ivor. Sahibs, Nabobs and Boxwallahs. *A Dictionary of the Words of Anglo-India*, New Delhi: Oxford University Press, 1997.

- Singh, Pashaura. *The Guru Granth Sahib, Canon, Meaning and Authority*, New Delhi: Oxford University Press, 2000, New Delhi: Oxford India Paperbacks, 2003.

History of Indian Literature in English

- Arvind, Krishna Mehrotra ed. *An Illustrated History of Indian Literature in English*, New Delhi: Permanent Black, 2003.

Essays

- Ashcroft, Bill *et al. The Empire Writes Back*, New York: Routledge, 1989.

- Holland, J. Nancy ed. *Feminist Interpretations of Jacques Derrida*, University Park, PA: Pennsylvania State University Press, 1997.

- Jain, Jasbir. *Writers of the Indian Diaspora. Theory and Practice,* Jaipur and New Delhi: Rawat Publications, 1998, 2003.

- Jakobsh, Doris, R. *Relocating Gender in Sikh History, Transformation, Meaning and Identity,* New Delhi: Oxford University Press, 2003.

- Khair, Tabish. Babu Fictions. *Alienation in Contemporary Indian English Novels,* New Delhi: Oxford University Press, 2001.

- Mukherjee, Meenakshi. *The Perishable Empire: Essays on Indian Writing in English,* New Delhi: 2000.

- Mukherjee, Meenakshi. *Midnight's Children, A Book of Readings,* New Delhi: Pencraft International, 2003.

- Narasinghaiah, C.D. ed. *Makers of Indian English Literature,* New Delhi: Pencraft International, 2000.

- Navati, U.M. and Kar, Prafulla, C. ed. *Rethinking Indian English Literature,* New Delhi: Pencraft International, 2000.

- Paniker, K. Ayyapa ed. *Indian English Literature Since Independence,* New Delhi: The National Indian Association for English Studies, 1991.

- Pathak, R.S. ed. *Quest for Identity in Indian English Writing,* Vol. I – *Fiction,* New Delhi: Bahri Publications, 1992.

- Ravi, P. S. Modern Indian Fiction: *History, Politics and the Individual in the Novels of Salman Rushdie, Amitav Ghosh,*

Upamanyu Chatterjee, New Delhi: Prestige Books, 2003.

- Said, Edward, W. *Orientalism, Western Conceptions of the Orient,* New York: Routledge and Kegan Paul, 1978, New Delhi: Penguin Books India, 2001.

- Said, Edward, W. *Culture and Imperialism,* London: Vintage, 1994.

Notes

Notes

Notes

Notes

Notes